LOCOMOTIVES OF THE VICTORIAN RAILWAY

THE EARLY DAYS OF STEAM

ANTHONY DAWSON

AMBERLEY

First published 2019

Amberley Publishing
The Hill, Stroud,
Gloucestershire, GL5 4EP

www.amberley-books.com

ISBN: 978 1 4456 7761 3 (print)
ISBN: 978 1 4456 7762 0 (ebook)

British Library Cataloguing in Publication Data.
A catalogue record for this book is available from the British Library.

Typeset in 10pt on 13pt Celeste.
Origination by Amberley Publishing.
Printed in the UK.

Contents

Introduction and Acknowledgements

This is not an exhaustive history of the locomotive; rather, it is a collection of essays examining particular locomotives which represent links in the chain of development between 1830 and *c.* 1850, each one represented by a preserved original locomotive or full-size working replica. While the locomotives of Robert Stephenson are prominent (Chapters 1 to 3), the work of Stephenson's major rival, Edward Bury, is included (Chapter 5), as well as that of Daniel Gooch on the broad gauge (Chapter 4).

Thanks are due to all those who have helped in the writing of this book: Andy Mason for his support of my literary endeavours; MRFS for editing and proofreading; David Boydell, Ian Hardman and Douglas Roberts for their photographs; Stephen Weston for his thoughts about Edward Bury; staff at the Museum of Liverpool; the Didcot Railway Centre; and to all those who built and have worked with *Planet*, to whom this book is respectfully dedicated.

CHAPTER 1

Rocket and her Kin

Rocket, the victor of the Rainhill Trials of October 1829, is perhaps one of the most famous railway locomotives in the world. She had been designed to do one thing: win at Rainhill, and while embodying the revolutionary boiler design of Henry Booth (1789–1869), the design would need refinement to improve efficiency running a timetabled main line passenger service. In essence, *Rocket* was a proof of concept and in fact, despite the replica *Rocket* regularly hauling passenger trains at the National Railway Museum and elsewhere, the original probably only did so rarely.

Rocket to Rainhill

Rocket was built by a consortium of father and son George (1781–1848) and Robert (1803–59) Stephenson and Henry Booth. George was the chief engineer of the Liverpool & Manchester Railway and Booth was the secretary and treasurer, and 'general superintendent' (in modern parlance, general manager) from 1833. Booth was a member of a prominent Liverpool merchant family and, like many of the Directors of the Liverpool & Manchester Railway, was a Unitarian. Booth was a champion of free trade, in favour of Parliamentary and social reform, was opposed to the Corn Laws and was instrumental in the introduction of Greenwich Mean Time. George Stephenson was a largely self-educated, hands-on engineer and mechanic. Determined to give his son the best possible start in life, Robert was educated at a Dissenting Academy in Newcastle, where he came to the attention of the Unitarian Minister Rev. William Turner (1761–1859) of Hanover Square Chapel. Apprenticed to Nicholas Wood (1795–1865) at Killingworth Colliery, Robert then attended the University of Edinburgh for two terms. With financial support coming from the Quaker Edward Pease (1767–1858), George Stephenson founded Robert Stephenson & Co. in 1823, the world's first purpose-built locomotive manufactory.

The Rainhill Trials had been established by the Liverpool & Manchester Railway Directors to ascertain whether locomotives or stationary engines would be the best means of operating their as yet unopened and unfinished railway. The suggestion to enter the Rainhill Trials came from Booth, and of the three serious contenders (*Rocket, Sans Pareil* and *Novelty*)

Above and opposite page: The remains of *Rocket* returned 'home' to Liverpool Road station (now part of the Science & Industry Museum in Manchester) from September 2018 to April 2019. Original components include the frames, boiler and cylinders; the driving wheels and valve-gear components are in-service replacements. The chimney is from the 1920s. (Ian Hardman)

The oldest known depiction of *Rocket*, drawn by Charles Vignoles for the *Mechanics' Magazine*, 24 October 1829.

Rocket was the only locomotive to have been built in a purpose-built locomotive factory, and to have had running-in trials to work out any 'teething troubles'.

The multi-tubular boiler of *Rocket* was Booth's design, apparently without knowledge of the contemporary work of Marc Séguin (1786–1875) in France, for whom Robert Stephenson & Co. had built two locomotives. The idea of a multi-tubular boiler was not new, however, having been first developed in France by the Marquis de Jouffory d'Abbans (1751–1832) for his steam boat built in 1784. *Rocket*'s boiler – which amazingly still exists after 190 years – is 6 feet long and 3 feet 4 inches in diameter. Of this boiler, Booth wrote:

> The problem to be solved was by what contrivance the largest quantity of steam could be raised in the shortest time, and in the smallest compass ... It struck me that a great point could be gained ... if instead of passing the fire through the boiler by means of one large iron tube ... we could carry the fire through a multitude of copper tubes only two or three inches in diameter ... We should obtain a much increased surface of heated metal exposed to the fire ... I mentioned my scheme to Mr Stephenson, and asked him if he would join me in building a locomotive to compete for the prize of 500L ... Mr Stephenson took a day or two to look into the merits of the plan ... and then told me he thought it would do, and join me in the venture. (Booth, 1980: 69)

Rocket's boiler is made from four plates of quarter-inch Staffordshire 'RB rolled iron' lap- and strap-riveted together. Running longitudinally through it are twenty-five copper pipes of 3-inch outside diameter. There were problems in getting the boiler steamtight: during August 1829 the 'clunking' of the tube endplates was a source of trouble and additional longitudinal stays had to be inserted to prevent the flat ends of the boiler bulging outwards.

The Rainhill Trials were re-enacted at the Llangollen Railway in 2002: *Rocket* is seen on shed raising steam together with *Sans Pareil* and *Novelty*. (Matthew Jackson)

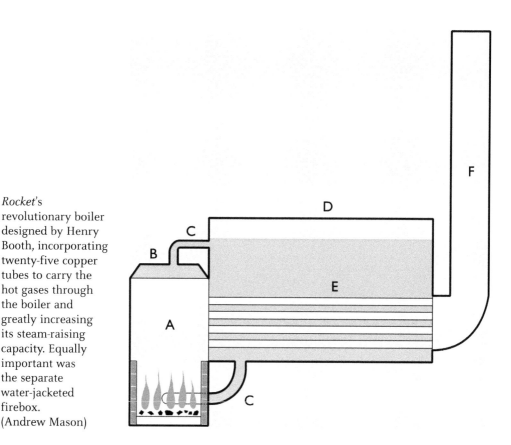

Rocket's revolutionary boiler designed by Henry Booth, incorporating twenty-five copper tubes to carry the hot gases through the boiler and greatly increasing its steam-raising capacity. Equally important was the separate water-jacketed firebox. (Andrew Mason)

Equally revolutionary was the firebox: prior to *Rocket* the fire had been formed on fire bars at one end of the main boiler flue, but in *Rocket* a separate, self-contained, water-jacketed firebox was provided. This gave ample room for flame development; its open bottom allowed a good throughput of air and the water jacket around the hottest part of the boiler made it an excellent steam generator.

Rocket had a pair of 8 x 16-inch cylinders mounted on iron plates at an angle of 38 degrees, driving a pair of wooden wheels (with iron hubs) 4 feet 8½ inches in diameter. Exhaust steam was carried from the cylinders through a pair of copper 'eduction pipes' to the base of the chimney, and thence via two nozzles on either side of the chimney. John Wesley Hackworth (1802–91), the embittered son of Stephenson's Rainhill rival, Timothy Hackworth, accused the Stephensons of stealing the idea of the blast pipe from his father. The blast pipe was not a new idea, however, as Richard Trevithick had first noted the effects of the blast pipe twenty-four years earlier.

Known as the 'flying reverse', *Rocket*'s valves are worked by slip eccentric valve gear. A pair of eccentrics are mounted between two cheek plates on the driving axle. A foot pedal on the foot plate works a Y-shaped yoke, which shifts the eccentric cluster to the right or left, engaging or disengaging a 'driving dog' clamped to the axle in a slot on the cheek plate. The eccentrics work a pair of eccentric rods, which in turn work a forward rocking shaft mounted on the front of the outer firebox. The motion for the valves is then carried up to cylinders via a pair of side levers; these levers terminate in a pair of drop-hooks which can

9

be locked or unlocked from pins on a pair of driving levers that work the valve spindles via a rocking shaft mounted on the back-head. By manually disengaging the drop-hooks the valves could be set – and worked – by hand. In order to slow down and reverse the locomotive, steam has to be shut off, the foot pedal unlocked (shifting the eccentrics over) and steam slowly reapplied, creating back pressure in the cylinders and causing the locomotive to come to a standstill before putting on more steam in order to move off in the opposite direction. Of this valve gear, Robert wrote: 'It is now as simple as I can make it and I believe effectual.'

As has often been told, *Rocket* won the Rainhill Trials and became the model for all future locomotives not only on the Liverpool & Manchester Railway, but across the world: a locomotive with a multi-tubular boiler; a proper firebox; and direct drive from cylinders to wheels.

Rocket's eccentric cluster. The two eccentrics (one per cylinder) are free to move laterally between a pair of driving dogs clamped to the axle to provide fore- and back-gear. (Matthew Jackson)

The eccentric rods feed back toward the footplate. The foot-pedal-operated yoke which shifts the eccentrics from side to side can also be seen.

Above left: Rocket's footplate: the polished valve handles are visible on the left, together with the foot-pedal and J-spring for reversing. (Lauren Jaye Gradwell)

Above right: Driver's eye view of the replica *Rocket*. The polished valve handles are constantly in motion as the locomotive runs, which is something the driver needs to be wary of. (Lauren Jaye Gradwell)

After Rainhill

Upon the conclusion of the trials, *Rocket* was taken to Liverpool and starred in a number of 'Public Relations exercises' running short trips along the partially completed line. From autumn 1829 *Rocket* was to be found in the far less glamorous task of working ballast trains on the Chat Moss contract, where the local press estimated she was saving the contractors at least £50 per month in horses, fodder and men. As soon as one line of rails was laid across the Moss, *Rocket* was used to prove to the doubters and sceptics that a locomotive and train could be run over it. The first run was on New Year's Day 1830, but after several successful runs over the Moss she came to grief propelling her train toward Eccles 'at a rate of twenty-four miles an hour'. One of her iron carrying wheels broke. The 'water carriage' and some of the wagons were thrown off but none of the 'forty individuals riding in and upon the wagons ... received the slightest hurt'. *Rocket*'s carrying wheels had been damaged before as the broken wheel and axle had 'been previously injured', *Rocket* having been 'purposely thrown off the railway'. *Rocket* was involved in further experiments on the Moss in April 1830 when she hauled a load of 45 tons, 'this being by far the greatest weight that has yet been conveyed across the Moss' – an area where only a few years ago man and horse feared to tread for becoming trapped. During this run *Rocket* attained a maximum speed of 16 mph.

Above left: The replica *Rocket* and a short train of replica contemporary first- and second-class carriages at Liverpool Road in 2010. (Matthew Jackson)

Above right: *Rocket* impatiently blows off steam at Liverpool Road, 2010. (Matthew Jackson)

Rocket was used in further public relations trips during the summer of 1830 in the lead-up to the grand opening that September, when she was involved in the accident to William Huskisson. She returned to ballast duties on Chat Moss a month later when she was involved in a second fatal accident: Henry Hunter, a local publican who had developed a habit, 'despite the repeated remonstrations of the Engineer', of hitching a ride on her tender from Ordsall Lane to Eccles. Sadly, as *Rocket* was propelling her train back to Manchester, one of the tender wheels broke, throwing Hunter from his perch. He was 'killed on the spot' by the 300-gallon water cask falling and crushing him.

Rocket was obsolete by New Year 1830 when the first of the improved 'Rocket type' locomotives ordered by the Liverpool & Manchester Railway was delivered. Because she was so underpowered compared to the later locomotives, *Rocket* does not appear to have been used in revenue-earning service and was variously used as a pilot engine, running ahead of the train in the dark to ensure no obstacles had been placed on the line, and as a ballast engine on permanent way duties. She was loaned to the Wigan Branch Railway in autumn 1832 (where she was damaged in an accident) and from the following year was used as a 'stand-by engine'. She was used as the testbed for Lord Dundonald's 'Rotary Engine' in 1833 and then laid up at the Edge Hill workshops until being sold on the behalf of the Earl of Carlisle in October 1836 for use on the Naworth Collieries railway.

Wildfire, Comet, Dart and *Arrow*

The Directors of the Liverpool & Manchester Railway ordered four locomotives of the Rocket type on 26 October 1829. They were to be delivered in three months, and, because of the lightly laid permanent way, were to weigh no more than 5 tons each. The *Morning Post* announced:

> The Directors of the Liverpool & Manchester Railway have ordered four locomotive engines on Mr Booth's Principle of Boiler, that of the 'Rocket' (which won the Prize of 500L) to be built by Messrs R. Stephenson & Co. (*Morning Post,* 17 November 1829).

These four locomotives were named *Wildfire* (later renamed *Meteor*), *Comet*, *Dart* and *Arrow*. They incorporated several lessons learned from *Rocket*. In order to increase the heating surface, the size of the boiler tubes was reduced from 3 to 2 inches outside diameter, and their number increased from twenty-five to ninety (*Arrow*) and ninety-two (*Meteor*). The boiler remained the same size as *Rocket*'s. A steam dome (*Rocket* had no dome at Rainhill) and an internal steam pipe (for greater thermal efficiency) were added. In order to prevent the unsteady, 'waddling' motion of *Rocket*, the cylinders (10 x 16 inches) were lowered from 38 degrees to 8 degrees, and driving wheels were increased to 5 feet in diameter. Although the Directors stated that the engines were to weigh no more than 5 tons each, *Arrow* weighed 5 tons 14 cwt 2 qr.

During her first trial run in January 1830, *Wildfire* certainly lived up to her name:

> The cylinders are larger, and placed almost horizontally, and the diameter of the wheels is four inches greater ... These alterations are expected to give the new engine greater speed, and to make its motion more regular and steady. There had also been an improvement made in means of stopping it, by which it may be brought to a standstill almost instantly ... it exhibited a grand and imposing sight...and, as the engine was approaching its maximum velocity, it continued to vomit out from the top of the chimney sparks, and masses of blazing coke, which gave the machine the appearance of a moving volcano, scattering fire-balls and red-hot cinders as it darted along the road, illuminating the air and throwing a transient glare on the countenances of the astonished bystanders ... aptly enough illustrated the name of 'Wildfire' which is given to it. (*Dublin Morning Register,* 22 January 1830)

Arrow underwent speed and load trials on 14 June 1830: drawing a load of 33 tons, she ascended the Whiston Incline (assisted by *Dart*) in 12 minutes, speed falling from 17 mph at the start of the climb to 4 mph at the summit. On the level she reached a maximum speed of 17 mph. On the return leg from Manchester to Liverpool, with only two passenger carriages, *Arrow* had an average speed of 20 mph and 'the whole distance was accomplished in 1 hour 46 minutes, including stoppages'. The Directors' Minutes record 'the rate of movement ... was frequently 25 miles per hour and upwards; the engine working below her power a great portion of the way'.

The First Smokebox

The success of *Wildfire* and her sisters led to two more locomotives being ordered on 1 February 1830: *Phoenix* and *North Star*. *Phoenix* was delivered by June 1830 and *North Star* in August. The cylinder diameter was increased from 10 to 11 inches, but the stroke (16 inches) remained unchanged. The boiler barrel was lengthened to 6 feet 6 inches. Unlike *Rocket*, *Phoenix* and *North Star* had a smokebox: a cylindrical extension of the boiler (probably about 18 inches long) with a narrow 'ash box' beneath, almost keyhole-shaped when viewed head on. There was a door to enable the tubes to be cleaned, a marked improvement on the earlier locomotives where the curved ducting at the base of the chimney was soon found to clog with ash, and had to be removed each time the tubes needed cleaning.

North Star was the next stage in development from *Rocket*, with larger cylinders, driving wheels and a larger boiler incorporating a smokebox. She was sold in 1834.

Phoenix (sister to *North Star*) was delivered in June 1830 and had a working life of just eighteen months or so, being broken up in October 1832.

Northumbrian

The final development of the 0-2-2 Rocket type was *Northumbrian*. While *Rocket* had brought together the essential elements of the locomotive boiler, it was in *Northumbrian* that the 'modern' boiler was first developed: a proper smokebox at the front end and a firebox contained within the boiler shell at the other. *Northumbrian* was also the first locomotive to use plate frames. *Northumbrian* was delivered on 31 July 1830 and cost £700 because of the 'increased quantity of copper, and superior workmanship of the engines, as now made'. While the *Mechanics' Magazine* states both the boiler and chimney were made from copper rather than iron, it is likely something has got garbled as a copper boiler would be extremely unlikely. It is more likely the inner firebox and tubes were copper and/ or that the boiler was sheathed with polished copper sheet, somewhat reminiscent of the 'tea urn' appearance of *Novelty*. Isaac Shaw saw and drew *Northumbrian* in 1831:

> It was built by Mr Stephenson ... and its construction is similar in its mechanical principles to the locomotive engine called the Rocket ... but some parts of the machinery are a little modified. The chief peculiarity in the construction is found in the addition of a branch tube from the waste steam-pipe to the bottom of the furnace, by opening a cock at the end of which the superfluous steam can be made occasionally to assist the combustion.
>
> The engine, mounted on four wooden wheels, having wrought iron rims, the diameter of the front being five feet, and that of the hind ... three feet. (Shaw 1831: 11–12)

The boiler barrel was 6 feet 6 inches long, 3 feet 4 inches diameter and contained 132 copper tubes 1⅝ inches outside diameter, giving a heating surface of 379 square feet. Shaw notes that the outer firebox was 3 feet 4 inches wide and 2 feet long. The inner firebox was copper, with the crown sheet supported by iron girders, and had a surface area of 36½ square feet. Shaw estimated that the boiler held 250 gallons of water, using 500 gallons

Northumbrian (August 1830) was the final development of the Rocket type and the first locomotive to have a modern 'locomotive type' boiler with a smokebox at one end and the firebox within the boiler barrel at the opposite.

A colourised version of James Nasmyth's famous sketch of *Northumbrian,* made on 12 September 1830, but which he incorrectly identified as *Rocket.*

Northumbrian as depicted by the *Mechanics' Magazine* in October 1830, with a curious rectangular smokebox.

of water between Liverpool and Manchester, and burning 4 cwt of coke. The steam dome was moved from the first ring of the boiler barrel to a position over the firebox, now on the hottest part of the boiler where the most steam was generated. This also meant that a relatively short steam pipe was needed, making for a more thermally efficient locomotive.

Frames

The Rocket type had wrought-iron bar frames. The main longitudinal frame members were 1 inch thick with 4-inch broad frames with transverse front and rear cross-members of the same dimensions. The frames are stepped down at the rear to support the firebox, but the back end of *Rocket*'s frames have risen up so that the footplate slopes towards the firebox, probably due to the lack of stiffening to support the weight of the firebox and the upward thrust of the carrying wheelset. As Bailey and Glithero have suggested, the introduction of wrought-iron stiffening rods between the firebox and footplate was an attempt to prevent this. Despite the presence of these bar frames, the boiler was considered the main structural element of the locomotive, to which everything was attached.

Rocket received additional 'supplementary frames' in 1831. These were fitted to not only strengthen the main frames, but to contain the thrust of the horn guides and also provide support for a buffer beam, which was probably added at the same date for greater operational flexibility. These supplementary frames – 1 inch by 4 inches – ran diagonally from the front of the frame to support the horn guides of the driving wheels. It is likely diagonal wrought-iron stays were fitted between the smokebox and leading end of the frames to stiffen that area. In order to lower the cylinders, cylinder mounting plates cut from solid ⅜ -inch-thick iron plate were added in February 1831.

Northumbrian's frames were a logical development: her main frame was made from inch-thick iron plate set on edge, which meant they were stronger under compression, and

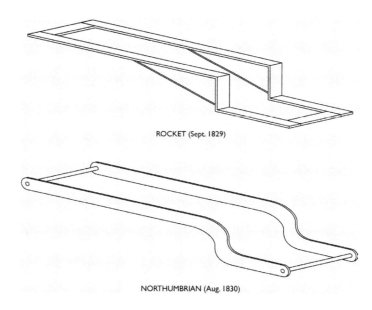

ROCKET (Sept. 1829)

The frames of *Rocket* (above) were a simple bar-frame composed of hand-forged iron bars while those of *Northumbrian* (bottom) were made from iron plates with tie-bars fore and aft, making it a more rigid construction. (Andrew Mason)

NORTHUMBRIAN (Aug. 1830)

17

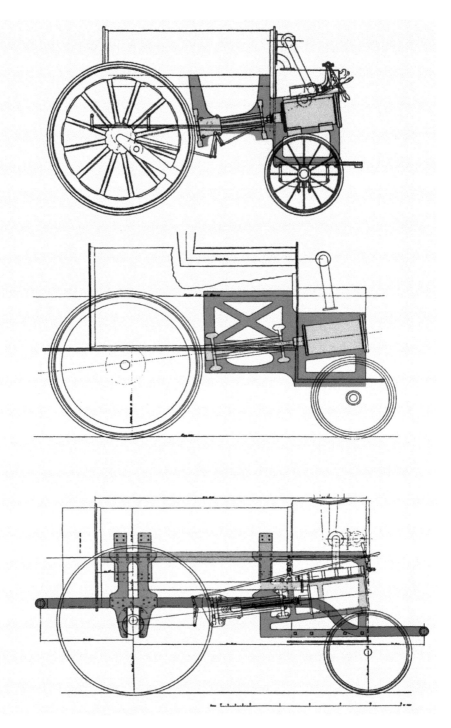

Arrow (top) (January 1830) had bar frames (red) and somewhat flimsy cylinder mounting plates (blue). The mounting brackets were extended with *Phoenix* (centre) (June 1830) to increase rigidity. *Northumbrian* (bottom) (August 1830) had plate frames (red) to which the cylinder brackets (blue) were riveted, together with the horn guides (orange). The boiler was supported on brackets (grey), which also stiffened the entire frame. (Andrew Mason)

joined at the front and rear via rolled iron tubes, through which passed a threaded iron bar, so that the whole assembly was bolted together. Each of the plates would have been hand-forged to shape. Cylinders were carried on plate iron mounting plates, lightened with cut-outs. The boiler and firebox were supported by three brackets: the first was riveted to the cylinder mounting plate, whilst the second and third were supported by the upper end of the driving wheel horn guides. The carrying wheels were carried in axle boxes riveted to the bottom of the firebox. The cylinders were mounted on large iron plates secured to the boiler and outer firebox. The next stage in development would be typified by *Planet*, with the adoption of outside sandwich frames (Chapter 2).

Delivery and Performance

The Directors' Minutes report *Northumbrian* was delivered at the beginning of August 1830, but the *Mechanics' Magazine* didn't record the fact until October. *Northumbrian* was chosen to pull the opening train of the Liverpool & Manchester Railway, hauling the magnificent carriage built for the Duke of Wellington on 15 September 1830, and it was on her tender that the mortally injured William Huskisson MP was carried to Eccles. She also pulled the first service train which ran the following day, when 150 Quakers journeyed from Liverpool to Manchester and back.

One correspondent reported that *Northumbrian* weighed 6 tons 3 cwt and was of 14 hp. Two Scottish civil engineers, Messrs Grainger and Buchanan, observed trials of *Northumbrian* on 16 and 17 September 1830 with a load of five passenger carriages:

From Liverpool to Manchester

		Mins.	Sec.
Greatest Speed	1 mile performed in	2	06
Slowest Speed		4	55
Average	20 miles	60	00

Back from Manchester to Liverpool

Greatest Speed	1 mile performed in	2	45
Slowest Speed		4	5̓7
Average	18 miles	60	00

In other words, *Northumbrian* was probably capable of speeds up to 30 mph. These times were 'exclusive of the time occupied in water at different points on the route'. Grainger and Buchanan also note that hot water was used to refill the tender. The *Mechanics' Magazine*, eager to repudiate the Stephensons, disputed these figures, claiming that *Northumbrian* was severely underpowered: in their opinion the passenger carriages weighed only 1½ tons rather than 4, so that the total load hauled by *Northumbrian* (five passenger carriages) claimed by Stephenson was in fact a mere 14 tons (including passengers). In fact, Grainger and Buchanan show *Northumbrian* was quite capable of drawing a load of 33 tons 6 cwt on

A non-working replica of *Northumbrian* was built by the LMS for the Railway Centenary of 1930; it is seen here in the paint shop at Derby Works.

the level and a load of 14 tons at 15 mph. The figures quoted by Grainger and Buchanan are supported by those given by Robert Stephenson in February 1831:

> The 'Northumbrian' drew 50 tons up the inclined planes at Rainhill at the average rate of 7½ miles per hour; pressure of steam 50 lbs on the square inch, inclination of the ground at Rainhill 1 in 96.

These engines had short working lives: *Comet* and *North Star* were sold to the civil engineer William Mackenzie, with *North Star* eventually going to the Leeds & Selby Railway. *Dart* was scrapped by 1833. It was proposed to rebuild *Phoenix* as a Planet-type in 1832 but she was scrapped and her boiler ended up as part of the feed water apparatus for the Edge Hill stationary engine. Lastly, *Majestic* was 'done with' by 1833 and *Northumbrian* three years later.

With *Northumbrian* the 0-2-2 locomotive had run its course, being superseded only months later by *Planet*. While retaining the same boiler design, *Planet* presented a radical departure in terms of layout: a 2-2-0 rather than 0-2-2 so that the smaller leading wheels helped guide the locomotive around curves, and with cylinders set low down at the front of the engine to further promote stability and faster running.

The replica of *Northumbrian* took a leading role in the Railway Centenary Celebrations held at Wavertree, near Liverpool, in September 1930.

In addition to *Northumbrian,* a replica of the opening train, including the impressive 'Ducal Car' used by the Duke of Wellington, was also built.

CHAPTER 2

Planet Suite

First steamed in 1992 in Manchester, and built by the Friends of the Museum of Science & Industry, the replica of Robert Stephenson's *Planet* represents the first 'modern' locomotive, and indeed the first mass-produced locomotive design. *Planet* incorporated design features which would become standard on locomotives for the next 130 years. As Dr Michael Bailey has stated, the delivery of *Planet* in October 1830 was the culmination of: 'An extraordinary period of research and development by Robert Stephenson and his close colleagues in the 33 months between January 1828 and September 1830' (Bailey 1997: 113).

Some forty members of the class were built, principally by Robert Stephenson & Co., but also by other makers under licence including Charles Tayleur & Co. of Newton-le-Willows and Fenton, Murray & Jackson of Leeds. 'Pirated' versions were also built in the United States.

The major innovations of *Planet* included:

- A boiler with an inner firebox as part of the boiler shell.
- A proper smokebox.
- A steam dome and internal steam pipe.
- Cylinders set low down at the front of the locomotive, working a cranked driving axle.
- The use of proper frames.
- The use of leaf springs, horns, and horn guides.

Moving the cylinders to a near-horizontal position at the front of the locomotive made the locomotive far more stable. The *Manchester Guardian* (4 March 1831) opined that:

> Though the engines constructed in this manner found to be very much more effective than any that had been previously in use, they still laboured under one obvious defect, by which their power was obviously impaired. As the two engines [cylinders], working out by alternate strokes, and communicated power to the *outsides of* the carriage, each stroke had a tendency to move that side of the carriage to which it was applied, at a quicker rate than the opposite side; the alternate advancing of the fore-wheels caused considerable unsteadiness of motion, which entirely disappeared when the steam was

Planet was the first main line express passenger locomotive, and forty or so examples were built worldwide. The working replica was built in Manchester and first steamed in 1992.

off ... In consequence of this defect, Mr Stephenson .... determined to try the effect of placing the cylinders beneath the boiler, and communicate the power to the wheels by means of two cranks in the axle ... This plan was reduced to practice in the construction of the *Planet,* and its consequences were immediately apparent in the steadiness of motion, and the very great working power of that engine ... We believe it was estimated that her effective power was nearly one-third greater than that of other engines of equal size, but made on the old principle.

By placing the cylinders beneath the smokebox, Stephenson increased their thermal efficiency, helping to reduce the formation of condensation, and therefore priming: something vitally important before the cylinder drain cock had been adopted.

While the boiler design of *Planet* was based upon that of *Northumbrian* – *Planet* was on the drawing board at the same time that *Northumbrian* was being constructed – the revolutionary part of the design was the cylinder position and crank axle. The use of a cranked driving axle was not new; Braithwaite & Ericsson's *Novelty* (1829) had a cranked driving axle, as did the steam road coaches of Goldsworthy Gurney.

Due to the technological limitations in producing a forged crank axle, Robert Stephenson took a 'belt and braces' approach: the axle was provided with outside bearings carried by the sandwich frames, but was also supported by four inside frames, which also served to carry the slide bars. Each of the inside frames carried a bearing so that the crank axle was supported on each side of the crank throws, relieving it of horizontal stresses, but only the outside bearings were sprung, the inside bearings simply being able to move vertically in guide boxes. Initially these inside frames were timber, but by 1832 these had been replaced by 'Iron axle rods', which are reported as 'answer[ing] very well'. These 'axle rods'

Fury, built for the Liverpool & Manchester Railway by Fenton, Murray & Jackson of Leeds in 1831.

A pirate Planet! *Bristol* was built by the Locks & Canals Company of Lowell, Massachusetts, in 1840 for the Western Railroad Company. Local modifications include a large spark-arresting chimney, a bell and a rudimentary cab.

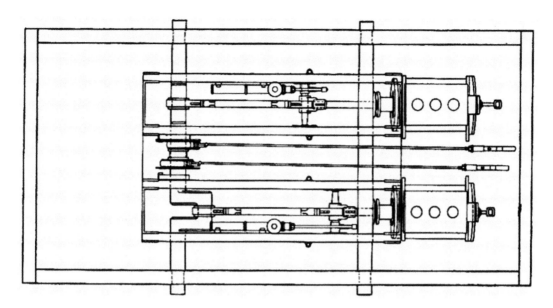

The frame of the Planet type was of composite construction, of ash timber sandwiched between two wrought-iron plates, with four intermediate frame members.

The view underneath the replica of *Planet* showing the outside sandwich frames and inside intermediate plate frames, which support the crank axle either side of the crank throws.

resembled connecting rods: they were fitted so as to accept brasses for the crank axle at one end, the opposite end being riveted to the cylinder block. These 'axle rods' were not load-bearing, and were hinged at the cylinder end to allow the axle to move vertically. By 1835 wrought-iron inside plate-frames had been introduced. They were riveted to the firebox and cylinder block, and again were not initially intended to be weight-bearing. The bearings were able to move vertically, but the outer pair were later provided with springs, presumably to relieve some of the stresses on the axle and outside bearings.

Wheels and Axles

The wheels of *Planet* were initially of composite construction: a cast-iron hub with ash spokes and oak felloes with a shrunk-on iron tyre. While these wheels had been successful enough on *Rocket* and *Northumbrian*, they were a failure on the earliest *Planet* types, which suffered from a series of broken wheels. *Pluto* was delivered in 1832 with wooden wheels, but *Ajax* (delivered November 1832) had iron. These composite wheels were replaced by early wrought-iron 'gas pipe' wheels in 1833, but these too were found to be prone to failure: the wheels of *Firefly, Eclipse* and *Star* collapsed, leading to the Liverpool & Manchester Board of Directors requesting a guarantee for wheels and axles from Stephenson & Co. and other manufacturers.

Before James Nasmyth invented the steam hammer, crank axles had to be forged by hand, and many of these early crank axles broke in service, often resulting in dangerous accidents. The axle of *Etna* broke in September 1831 and that of *Fury* in December 1831. It wasn't just the Liverpool & Manchester Planets which suffered from this problem, however: *Nelson* (Leeds & Selby) also broke her crank axle. This was due to poor axle design: the diameter of the axle was stepped-down for insertion into the wheel hub, and further stepped-down for the outside bearing journals. Unfortunately, the radii on the shoulder of the axle, where the axle stepped down in diameter, were prone to stress fractures due to the radii being too small, and from a lack of stress-relieving grooves machined into the axle. Replication repeated history as the replica *Planet* suffered from two broken axles, with stress fractures caused in exactly the same location as the originals.

The Directors of the Liverpool & Manchester ordered new, thicker axles to be introduced in December 1831 and a new design was duly produced which introduced a continuous diameter through the wheel-hub. These new axles 'of Swedish Iron or of English Iron smelted with wood charcoal' were 5 inches in diameter (compared to 4½ of the previous design), and 'very heavy and very expensive costing £50 each'. After the crank axle of *Pluto* failed in September 1833, the Directors expected 'a guarantee of the soundness of the wheels and axles for twelve months' from Stephenson & Co.

The Chevalier de Pambour in 1835 shows that even stronger crank axles had been introduced, and the axle increased from 5 inches diameter to 5½ inches diameter where it passed through the wheel hub. De Pambour also shows collars fitted to each end of the crank axle. These collars were to prevent lateral spread of the horn guides as the locomotive travelled around sharp curves: the 1992 replica of *Planet* originally displayed this same problem, especially in reverse, so that collars were subsequently fitted to the axle in order to cure this lateral spread. In his design for his Patent Locomotive of 1833

Detail of *Planet*'s 'gas pipe' driving wheel, horn guide and axle box. The first Planets suffered from wheel breakages until a durable design was developed by Stephenson & Co.

(Chapter 3), Robert Stephenson introduced and patented flangeless driving wheels in order to 'obviate or diminish' the lateral spread on the crank axle by allowing greater lateral movement of the driving wheels.

The problems with making robust crank axles led to George Forrester (1781–?) of Liverpool abandoning them entirely, introducing outside-cylinder locomotives, as did Joseph Locke (1805–60) and William Barber Buddicom (1816–87) on the Grand Junction Railway. Repeated failure of crank axles of the 2-2-2 Patentee type locomotives (Chapter 3) traversing the sharp curves where the Grand Junction joined the Liverpool & Manchester led to the development of the outside-cylinder 'Crewe Type' in 1839–41. These were built as both 2-2-2 and 2-4-0s as the mainstay of the LNWR Northern Division. The name 'Crewe Type' is something of a misnomer, however, as Crewe Works did not originate the design; rather, it was developed at Edge Hill. Also known as the 'Allan Type', the actual involvement of Alexander Allan (1809–91) was minimal. *Columbine*, built in Crewe in 1845, and now on display at the Science Museum, is a rare survivor of this once ubiquitous, and long-lived, class. A similar design was introduced on the Caledonian Railway and the Highland Railway. With Buddicom moving to France in 1840, he took the design with him, where it became known as 'La Buddicom' and many of these little engines were at work into the twentieth century. *St Pierre*, which is on display at *Cité du Train* (the French national railway museum at Mulhouse), is the earliest surviving example of a 'Crewe Type' locomotive.

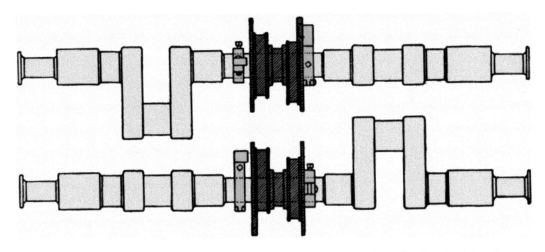

The design of the crank axle evolved over time to the form shown here by the Chevalier de Pambour. Note the eccentric cluster (red), which was free to move laterally between the driving dogs (blue) and the end collars to prevent lateral spread of the horn guides.

Columbine, built at Crewe in 1845, is the sole UK survivor of the once numerous 'Crewe Type'. (Ian Hardman)

A typical example of the 'Crewe Type' developed by Joseph Locke and William Barber Buddicom.

St Pierre, a surviving French example of the 'Crewe Type' – or 'Buddicoms' as they are known in France – was built at Chartreux in 1843 for the Chemin de Fer Paris à Rouen. She is the oldest surviving example of the type.

Making Steam

To return to the 1830s, *Planet*'s boiler was based on that for *Northumbrian*, being 6 feet 6 inches long and 3 feet 3 inches in diameter and containing 129 copper tubes of 1⅝-inch outside diameter. By using so many tubes, Stephenson had restricted water circulation within the boiler; using a larger diameter boiler barrel and fewer tubes (under 100) solved this problem. The firebox had a surface area of 37¼ feet and the tubes provided a heating surface of 370 square feet – 407¼ square feet in total – and was an excellent steam generator. Even though Stephenson had provided outside 'Sandwich frames', the boiler was considered to be a major structural element of the locomotive and was rigidly fixed to the frames, and was therefore unable (or at least restricted) in its ability to expand when it was pressurised. Furthermore, the drag pin was riveted directly to the rear of the firebox shell, which meant that the load was passed not through the frame but the boiler. This was a major design flaw, resulting in the only boiler explosion on the L&M – that of *Patentee* in 1838 (Chapter 3).

Due to the limitations of forging wrought-iron plates much larger than 4 feet by 3 feet, the boiler and outer firebox was made from more than twenty iron plates ⅜ inches thick and measuring 4 feet 1 inch by 3 feet 1 inch. The boiler plates were lap riveted together; where the smokebox and firebox shell met the boiler barrel, angle irons were used. Because of the high cost of copper, the inner firebox was iron, but they were very rapidly found to 'burn out'; firebox tube plates are recorded as having caused considerable trouble, including buckling due to overheating. This was probably due to poor water circulation around the inner firebox due to the build-up of scale and sludge, especially between the tube plate and the front of the outer firebox shell which, unusually, was not provided with any mud hole doors to enable that part of the firebox to be cleaned out. Experiences

The replica of *Planet* impatiently blows off at the Science and Industry Museum, with Peter Brown (driver) and Mike Ward (fireman) expertly at the helm.

with the replica *Planet* show this area is very prone to scale and sludge deposition. Some locomotives such as *Fury* had gone through three fireboxes in only two years; the first firebox lasted for 21,330 miles and the second – made from Low Moor iron – a mere 6,060. Clearly, iron fireboxes were not the way forward; at the suggestion of the L&M's engineer, John Dixon, the fireboxes were changed to copper in 1833.

The copper tubes were quickly found to wear out, due to coke ash being particularly abrasive. In an attempt to cure this, thicker copper tubes were used experimentally, but to little avail. Finally, in December 1833 hard-wearing brass tubes were adopted. There were obviously problems with water circulation in the boiler, as in April 1833 the L&M Management Sub-Committee ordered all future engines should have 'the tubes ... placed further apart' to increase water circulation in the boiler, and prevent tubes from overheating.

The regulator was located under the dome (mounted over the firebox) and the main steam pipe ran the length of the boiler. Unusually, it branched to supply steam to both cylinders within the boiler barrel, rather than in the smokebox. This was simply due to lack of space within the small smokebox of the *Planet* (and *Samson*) design.

The boiler was fed with two cross-head-driven feed pumps, which meant that water could only be put into the boiler while the locomotive was moving. There is no primary evidence to support the oft-quoted myth that early locomotives like *Planet* were run up to a buffer stop, the rails greased and the engine set running to pump water into the boiler. In order to overcome this disadvantage (and to enable the fireman to stop the locomotive from blowing off), the replica *Planet* has a single injector as well as a feed pump.

Planet – and all other locomotives on the Liverpool & Manchester – had a usual maximum working pressure of 50 psi. Two safety valves were provided: one of Salter type which also acted as a crude pressure gauge and a second spring-loaded valve placed out of reach of the engineman, locked up in a brass casing 'to prevent him from overloading this valve, as he is often tempted to do so in order to obtain from the engine a greater effect, even at the risk of danger' (Pambour, 1840: 47).

In the opinion of the Chevalier de Pambour, the calibration of these valves was imperfect:

> It sometimes happen that ... the pressure is declared to be 50 lbs per square inch, while it really is 60 or 70 lbs. Moreover, the calculation of the pressure is generally so incorrectly made, that any dependence cannot be placed upon it. (Pambour, 1840: 47)

De Pambour also states that an L&M fireman was not thought to be doing his job properly unless the safety valves were constantly blowing off, and quite rightly thought this very wasteful of fuel (coke) and water.

Valve Gear

The valve gear on *Planet* was based on that used by *Rocket* (and her successors) and *Northumbrian:* slip-eccentric with manual override.

As with *Rocket*, a pair of eccentrics are sandwiched between a pair of cheek plates, mounted on a sleeve on the crank axle. These are free to move laterally on the axle between

Left: Detail of *Planet*'s eccentric cluster and yoke arrangement, which shift the eccentrics between the pair of driving dogs. (Matthew Jackson)

Below: *Planet*'s reverser laid out in working position, showing the arrangement of the foot pedal and its associated rodding, yoke and the eccentrics. (Matthew Jackson)

a pair of driving dogs. These dogs were at first clamped to the axle, but in April 1833, following an accident due to inoperative valve gear because the drivers had slipped, it was ordered 'that the Excentric Drivers should be tapped fast into the Axle Shaft, so that once set right they might not be liable to get wrong, as they frequently did, either from accident or design' (RAIL 371/8).

Each of the cheek plates has a slot into which one of the driving dogs engages; the whole eccentric assembly is shifted from left to right via a yoke, controlled from the footplate by a pedal. When the pedal is pushed down, the yoke shifts to the right, engaging forward gear. When it is disengaged, the yoke moves to the left, engaging reverse gear. The foot pedal was originally kept in place with a J-spring but on the replica this was replaced by a torsion-bar system, which proved far more reliable. Stephenson described this arrangement in great detail:

> Two eccentrics ... fixed together at right angles to each other, and placed loose upon the centre of the cranked axle ... and a driver with a projecting stud is fixed on the axle on each side, just clearing the eccentrics, a hole being made in each side of the eccentrics to fit the studs. The eccentrics can be shifted along the axle to either side by means of a lever, to make the stud in the driver on that side drop into the hole on the eccentric when it comes opposite to it in revolving, and cause the eccentric to turn with the axle and work the slides. The stud of the driver is put on the opposite side of the axle to the corresponding hole in the eccentric; so that when the eccentrics are shifted to the other side by the lever, they have to stop half a revolution before the driver catches hold of them, and are then fixed exactly opposite to their former position, and reverse the engine; in their intermediary position, when they touch neither of the drivers, they are stationary and cease to work the slides. (Marshall, 1838: 45)

The eccentrics drive a pair of eccentric rods – one per cylinder – and pass forward between the cylinders. Each of the eccentric rods terminates in a drop-hook. These drop-hooks engage with a pin on the forward rocking shaft which drives the valve spindles. They can be raised and lowered from the footplate via a lifting link so that they are either engaged and locked in place, driving the rocking shaft, or disengaged, leaving the valve gear free to be worked by hand.

When unlocked, the valves can be worked manually from the footplate using two 'valve levers' on the left-hand side of the footplate. These control the front rocking shaft; the left-hand lever controls the left-hand valve and the right-hand lever the right-hand valve. Furthermore, the movement of the levers follows that of the valves themselves. When the lever is pushed forward, the valve moves forward, uncovering the rear steam port. In order to start the locomotive it was usual to drive the locomotive 'on the handles'. Driving 'on the handles' provides 100 per cent cut-off – in other words, maximum boiler pressure to the pistons in the cylinders. There is a lot of skill and practice required in driving the locomotive on the handles. When the locomotive has begun to move and gained momentum by being driven manually, the eccentrics can be engaged: the drop-hooks can be lowered on to the drive pins on the front rocking shaft and the locomotive will run on its own. Isaac Watt Boulton said of this valve gear:

> My old friend, whom I had known as a lad, from stationary winding engine driver, then as a fireman, and he soon became engineman, then night foreman, and at the time I spoke to him, as second-in-command of the locomotive department ... I saw this old friend get on [the] locomotive with two loose excentrics and hand gear ... He tried hard for a long time to get it to move, but had to give it up. He could not get her to move in either

The footplate of the replica *Planet* is somewhat more complicated than the original. The valve levers which shift the valves manually are on the left with the foot pedal (for the reverser) just visible through the footplate. Modern refinements include two sight glasses, a blower and an injector to put water back into the boiler.

direction. When another old friend – Old Bill [William Holmes, driver of *Planet*] – who did understand the hand gear, got on, and off she went in a jiffy. I have often started a load with the loose-excentric gear, while the same engine could not start it off with the fixed-excentrics. You could give the engine the steam, full on the piston, the *instant* the crank passed the centre – that is, if you knew how. (*The Engineer*, 7 November 1884)

In order to stop the locomotive, the regulator would be closed, shutting off steam. As the locomotive drifts to a halt, the reverser pedal can be disengaged (if the locomotive is travelling forwards) to put the locomotive into reverse. Because the locomotive is still moving forward, but with the regulator closed and valve gear in reverse, steam can be gently admitted into the cylinders, creating back-pressure to slow down and stop the locomotive. With skill and practice a locomotive can be gently brought to a stand and be held stationary on the regulator. Although the replica of *Planet* has a modern air-brake system, her drivers take pride in being able to stop and start her in 1830s style.

Planet, coupled to a short train of 'period' rolling stock, including the restored 1840s Manchester & Birmingham coach, is seen ready to depart in January 2016.

Engine Builders

Robert Stephenson & Co. delivered one locomotive per month throughout 1831 for the Liverpool & Manchester Railway, but were obviously unable to cope with such an influx of orders. Three Planet-type locomotives were built in Leeds by Fenton, Murray & Jackson of the 'Round Foundry' – the oldest locomotive building firm in the business, having constructed the four Murray-Blenkinsop engines for the Middleton Railway in 1812. The rush to get locomotives built was quickly seen in several locomotives which were not 'fit for purpose' upon delivery, including *Atlas*, *Milo* and *Vesta*. This poor build quality was due to rushed work, but also because Stephenson & Co. lacked machine tools. As Dr Richard Hills has identified:

> While [they had] ... so dramatically inaugurated the development of the locomotive, they seem to have failed to upgrade their production facilities. (Hills, 2003: 255)

In 1823 Stephenson & Co. had purchased a 'pair of Smith's Bellows, Anvils, Vices' and '3 lathes'. Even as late as 1837 the firm had failed to introduce machine tools – or indeed machinery:

> There was not a single crane in Robert Stephenson's shop ... There were shear-legs in the yard, by which a boiler could be lifted onto a truck, and there were portable shear-legs in the shop, by the skilful manipulation of which, at no little risk of life and limb, wonders were done in the way of transmitting heavy loads from one part of the shop to another. And the only steam-engine in that which was the most important locomotive shop in the world ... was a vibrating pillar machine, with a single 16 inch cylinder and 3 feet stroke. (Hills, 2003: 255)

Robert Stephenson & Co. was established on Forth Street, Newcastle-upon-Tyne, as the world's first locomotive manufacturer in 1823. The firm merged with Hawthorn Leslie after more than a century of operation, in 1937.

The Stephensons even lagged behind the works of the Liverpool & Manchester at Edgehill, where John Melling had access to 'sundry Machines for punching boiler plates, Planing Slides, Boring Cylinders etc.' as well as a hydraulic wheel press and a lathe for turning wheels and axles. Forth Street was 'poorly equipped ... [with] great reliance on the blacksmith'. Instead of working drawings, locomotives were drawn in chalk in full size and parts were made to fit this full-size drawing, probably with quite a bit of fettling and fitting during actual construction. It's little wonder that despite the L&M Directors ordering a pair of locomotives be identical to allow for interchangeability of parts, that wasn't the case: each and every engine was a hand-made one-off. The transition from short colliery lines to main line railways demanded production and maintenance facilities which were more than just a blacksmith's shop – something the Stephensons had failed to grasp at this early period.

In contrast to the work taking place at Newcastle, Fenton, Murray & Jackson (and their antecedents, Fenton, Murray & Wood) of Leeds had been using machine tools for decades in building mill machinery and steam engines in a well-equipped workshop. They were:

> Manufacturers of the most established reputation ... The engines they send out cannot be excelled in beauty and perfection of workmanship; and they perform as well as any others. Their factory at Leeds is very extensive, and provided with every convenience for making all the part of the engine in the best manner, and with the least labour. They have three steam-engines in the works, one for boring cylinders and turning large wheels; second for turning small lathes, grinding, drilling the centres of wheels, tapping screws etc.; and for blowing the furnaces of the foundry; and a third engine for working a great forge hammer. (Hills: 251)

Replica
builder's plate
on *Planet*.

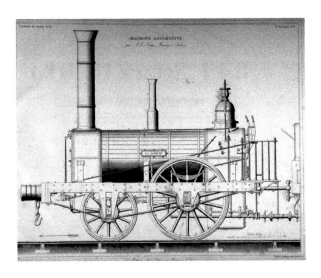

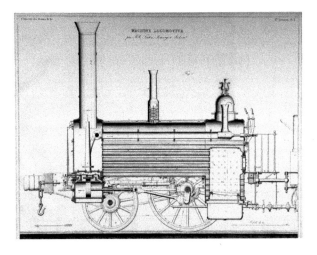

La Jackson, built by Fenton, Murray & Jackson of Leeds for the Chemin de Fer de Paris à Saint Germain in 1834. A 'typical' member of the Planet class from the mid-1830s.

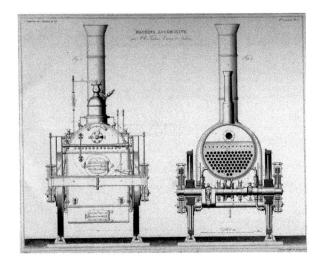

French commentators note that while being very robust, that locomotives built by Stephenson & Co. had a poor build quality, especially compared to the products of Fenton, Murray & Jackson of Leeds. There was no standardisation or interchangeability of parts. Similarly, the products of the Atlas Works of Sharp, Roberts & Co. on Bridgewater Street, Manchester, far surpassed anything produced at Forth Street in terms of build quality and standardisation of parts and fixings. Roberts & Co. also pioneered the use of proper working drawings. According to Dr Richard Hills, Richard Roberts (1789–1864) 'had recognised the need for improving the quality of workmanship in locomotives ... and used his engineering ability to produce high quality products' (Hills & Patrick, 1982: 9). By the late 1830s, newer companies such as the Atlas Works 'began to rival the older firm of Robert Stephenson & Co.' with a 'most distinguished reputation' for the design, workmanship and standardisation of their locomotives compared to the products of Forth Street.

Delivery and Performance

Planet was completed on 3 September 1830, just twelve days before the Liverpool & Manchester Railway was to be opened by the Duke of Wellington. She was delivered by sea to Liverpool on 4 October 1830, although rumour suggests she had been ready for the opening day of the L&M (15 September) and had been stranded onboard the ship. Numbered 9 in the L&M fleet, *Planet* underwent running trials during October and November. The *Manchester Courier* on Saturday 9 October 1830 reported the arrival of *Planet* and the rumour that she had run the 30 miles between Liverpool and Manchester in a record-breaking time of 32 minutes. A time of 1 hour 32 minutes is more likely, given that she is recorded on 23 November 1830 as having made the same run in 60 minutes, which included 2 minutes 'taken up in examining and oiling the machinery':

> Liverpool to Manchester in One Hour – It has often been a subject of doubt whether the distance from Liverpool to Manchester could be travelled by a Locomotive engine in the space of one hour; this extraordinary feat was performed on Monday morning by the Planet, one of Mr Stephenson's most approved engines, the time occupied being only 60 minutes, of which 2 minutes were taken up in oiling and examining the machinery about midway. There were no carriages attached to the Engine, the only persons on the Tender being the Engineer, the Fireman, and Mr Williams, the Principal Clerk, in Crown-Street Station. The occasion of this rapid passage was the necessity for the Engine being in Manchester by nine o'clock a.m., it having been engaged by Mr Ewart's Committee to bring down the Duke's train with the Manchester voters, and some alteration in her machinery being unexpectedly required, she was prevented setting out until the latest moment, and the Engine at the other end were all occupied with the regular business of the road. (*Gore's Liverpool General Advertiser*, 25 November 1830)

On 29 November the Directors ordered 'a trial of the power of the 'Planet' Engine be made', hauling a load of goods between Liverpool & Manchester. The experiment was a success, as the *Liverpool Mercury* (Friday 10 December 1830) reported:

The replica of *Planet* in an almost period view, standing outside the '1830 Warehouse' at Liverpool Road. (David Boydell)

Extraordinary Performance on the Railway. On Saturday last, the Planet locomotive engine (one of Mr. Stephenson's) took the first load of merchandise which has passed along the Railway from Liverpool to Manchester. The train consisted of some 18 waggons, containing 135 bags and bales of American cotton, 200 barrels of flour, 63 sacks of oatmeal, and 35 sacks of malt, what weighing altogether 51 tons 11 cwt. I qr. To this must be added the weight of the waggons and oil cloths, viz. 23 tons 8 cwt. 3 qrs; tender, water, end fuel 4 tons, and of 15 persons upon the train, 1 ton, making a total weight of exactly eighty tons, exclusive of the engine, about six tons. The journey was performed in 2 hours end 54 minutes, including three stoppages of five minutes each (one only being necessary under ordinary circumstances) for oiling, watering, and taking in fuel; under the disadvantages also of an adverse wind, and of a great additional and friction in the wheels and axles, owing to their being entirely new. The train was assisted up the Rainhill inclined plane, by other engines, at the rate of 9 miles an hour, and descended the Sutton incline at the rate of l6 miles an hour. The average rate on the other parts of the road was 12 miles an hour, the greatest speed on the level being 15 miles an hour, which was maintained for a mile or two at different periods of the journey ... Taking this performance as a fair criterion, which there is no reason to doubt, four engines of the same class as the Planet, (with the assistance of one large engine, constructed for the purpose, up the inclined plane) would be capable of taking upon the Railway all the cotton which passes between Liverpool and Manchester.

Hardman Earle reported back to the Directors on 6 December 1830:

The first load of Merchandise by the Railway from Liverpool to Manchester had been sent by the 'Planet' Locomotive in 18 Waggons, on Saturday the 4th instant ... the Nett Weight chargeable with freight was 51 Tons 1 cwt; the Gross Weight drawn by the engine, including Waggons, Tender and Passengers, being about 80 tons. The journey was accomplished in 6 minutes less than 3 hours, including stoppages for water and oiling. (RAIL 371/2)

Planet was obviously a success and orders were placed in 1830 with Robert Stephenson & Co. for two additional locomotives, to be named *Mercury* and *Mars. Jupiter, Saturn, Sun, Venus, Etna, Victory* and *Vesta* followed in 1831 from Newcastle while Fenton, Murray & Jackson of Leeds supplied *Vulcan, Fury* and *Leeds*. The *Chester Chronicle* recorded *Fury*'s delivery:

A Beautiful new locomotive engine, 'The Fury', of Mr Stephenson's construction, was 'launched' at Liverpool on the Liverpool & Manchester Railway on Wednesday week, making the number now in operation amount to eighteen; and the number of passengers during the present week, has averaged about 2000 per day! (*Chester Chronicle*, 3 June 1831)

In service, the Planet class proved to be fast, reliable and fuel-efficient: by 1 April 1833 *Planet* had run 41,400 miles, far more than other members of her class. Experiments were carried out using the newly delivered *Victory* in May 1832. On 5 May:

This engine drew from Liverpool to Manchester ... in 1 hour, 34 minutes, 75 seconds, twenty loaded waggons, weighing gross, 92 tons, 19 cwt, 1 qr.; consumption of coke 929lbs net.; was assisted on the Rainhill incline plane 1 1/2mile by the Samson. The fire-place was filled with coke at the starting (not weighed), and was again filled with coke on arriving at Manchester; the coke used in getting the steam up was not used in the above estimate. (*Edinburgh Review*, cited by *Wolverhampton Chronicle*, 19 December 1832)

With this load, *Victory* achieved a speed of 20 mph on the dead level, rose to 25.5 mph on a falling gradient and on a rising gradient she achieved 17 mph. On 8 May, and with a load of twenty wagons weighing 90 tons 7 cwt 2 qrs gross, *Victory* made the same trip in 1 hour 41 minutes, including a lengthy stop of 11 minutes for water and oiling round. Despite a severe headwind, she made a maximum speed on the level of 17.7 mph, but one of her big-end bearings ran hot, and 'upon arriving at Manchester, pistons found so loose in the cylinder that steam blew through'.

The heating surface of *Planet* was greater than the earlier Rocket types: *Planet* burned 19¾ lb of coke per 30-mile trip while *North Star* was burning 10 lbs more. Comparative trials ordered by the L&M board showed *Planet* burned 0.48 lb of coke per ton per mile (or 839 lb per trip), showing her to be remarkably fuel-efficient.

The Planet class – and its 0-4-0 Samson derivative – was the first mass-produced 'class' of locomotives and was the progenitor of the main line steam locomotive for the next 130 years; to paraphrase former NRM Director Colonel Steve Davies, *Planet* was the locomotive equivalent of the space shuttle compared to *Rocket*'s Apollo 11. Hardman Earle thought that with the *Planet* design the steam locomotive had come as close to perfection as it was then possible (1832):

It is now two years since the Planet was laid down, and upwards of twenty engines have since been launched from the Newcastle and other manufactories, and yet she comes nearer to what we consider perfection (relative, of course) than any which have succeeded, but her form and general construction has never been improved upon.

Planet was the first true main line express passenger locomotive, but in order to meet the demands of increased loads and speed, and also to maintain a low axle weight, a larger locomotive on six wheels was needed. The answer was Robert Stephenson's *Patentee*.

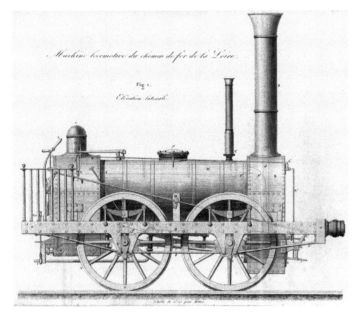

Left: The next logical step in the evolution of the locomotive was the 0-4-0 Samson type; its kinship with the 2-2-0 Planet type is clearly evident.

Below: The replica of *Planet* in company with two replica Liverpool & Manchester second-class coaches and the original Manchester & Birmingham coach (*c.* 1842). (Matthew Jackson)

CHAPTER 3

Patent Locomotives

Perhaps best known as the *Titfield Thunderbolt*, Liverpool & Manchester Railway No. 57 *Lion*, built by the enigmatic Leeds firm of Todd, Kitson & Laird in 1838, is a unique survivor of the Liverpool & Manchester Railway, and was built to two patents: those of Robert Stephenson (7 October 1833) and John Melling (26 July 1837).

Robert Stephenson's six-wheel locomotive was a logical evolution from the 2-2-0 Planet type; by providing an extra pair of wheels behind the firebox he helped prevent a phenomenon known as 'hunting' and was able to fit a larger firebox than before. The main design criteria of *Patentee* were:

- Better weight distribution through provision of extra carrying wheels.
- Flangeless driving wheels to relieve the crank axle of lateral stresses.
- Larger firebox and boiler.
- Easier to manage 'Gab' valve gear.
- Slide valves with limited 'lap' and 'lead' to improve fuel efficiency.
- Main steam pipe bifurcating in the smokebox (and provision of a smokebox door).
- Efficient braking on the locomotive via a steam brake.

The design had several teething problems, especially with Stephenson's patent 'Gas Pipe' wheels, crank axles and weight distribution. In his wheel design, Stephenson utilised hollow, wrought-iron spokes, offset like those on a bicycle, with a cast-iron nave and rim. The wheels were then turned on a lathe and wrought-iron tyres were shrunk on, and then bolted in place. They did not, however, prove durable in service as the cast-iron rims were found to be very brittle and prone to breakage – so much so that the Liverpool & Manchester Directors ordered in February 1834 their use be suspended, and the patent wheels of Richard Roberts & Co. of Manchester or Edward Bury of Liverpool be adopted instead. Roberts had patented his locomotive wheel in 1833, using a solid cast-iron wheel, with a separate wrought-iron tyre which was shrunk on after the rim had been turned to size. He later used wrought-iron spokes which were assembled in place, and then a cast-iron hub was poured around them and the tyre shrunk on. Edward Bury's wheels are discussed on pages 82–3. The Board also stipulated that locomotive manufacturers should

Lion, alias *Thunderbolt* from the Ealing comedy *The Titfield Thunderbolt*, was resident at the Science & Industry Museum in Manchester between 1999 and 2007. (David Boydell)

guarantee their wheels for 50,000 miles before they accepted them.

Adoption of 'gab' gear made driving considerably easier. Instead of using two loose eccentrics, he provided four fixed eccentrics: two eccentrics per valve, one for fore-gear and the second for back-gear. Due to limited space between the frames, the fore-gear eccentrics were placed on the crank axle, either side of the Y-shaped frame stay, while those for back-gear were squeezed between the inside plate frames and outer sandwich frames. Each of the eccentric rods terminated in an upward-facing V-shaped gab that could be raised or lowered from a single lever from the footplate to engage with a pin on a rocker arm, for forward or reverse gear. It could thus:

Be made to run either forward or backward, by merely pulling the hand lever forward or back; and the handle is placed closed to the engine man, who stands behind the firebox, so as to be readily moved. (Marshall, 1838: 44)

The introduction of 'lap' and 'lead' to the valves – lap is the amount by which the valve overlaps the steam port at the middle position of each valve and lead is the amount by which the steam port is open when the piston is at dead-centre – gave for a much freer exhaust, so that the used steam escaped quicker, reducing back-pressure in the cylinders, helping the locomotive to run faster due to not being 'throttled'.

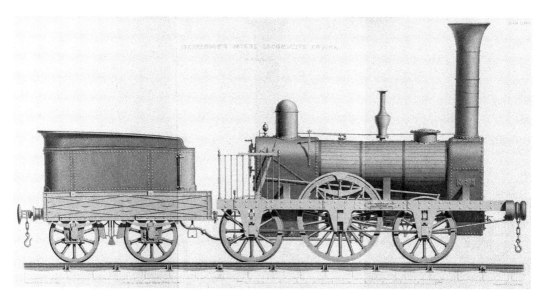

Robert Stephenson's six-wheel engine of 1833 was designed to reduce the axle load on the lightweight permanent way then in use on the Liverpool & Manchester Railway, and to provide greater stability at speed. It also allowed the use of a larger boiler and firebox.

Patentee

Thus, Robert Stephenson's 'Patent Locomotive' contained numerous improvements over the Planet class: *Patentee* had in fact been built speculatively by Stephenson & Co. She underwent trials on the Liverpool & Manchester in April and May 1834. She originally had flanged driving wheels, which were found to damage the permanent way, in particular the switches. She was offered to the Liverpool & Manchester for £1,000 in July 1834 on the condition that she be fitted with 'new cylinders and frame work ... to strengthen the fastenings of her interior framing', with Stephenson & Co. 'being responsible for any repairs that might be suggested'. As a result, she was sent to Charles Tayleur & Co. to have the flanges removed from the driving wheels and following this modification was accepted in to stock in September 1834. The first locomotives to run in Germany and Belgium were Patentees.

Patentee had a chequered career: on 29 March 1836 she ran into the *Leeds*, which was crossing out of the 'pig siding' at Manchester. A month later her front axle broke near Bury Lane while working the 5 p.m. first class train, and she ran off the rails. Henry Booth was instructed to investigate and concluded that the accident had been made worse because the driving wheels lacking flanges meant that they could not hold the locomotive on the track in case of a similar accident in the future. As a result she was fitted with flanged driving wheels.

In January 1838 *Patentee* collided with *Phoenix* on the Whiston Incline; then in April her fireman, Daniel McVie, was crushed to death while disconnecting the tender water hoses; in October she was involved in a fatal accident at Newton Junction. Finally, in November

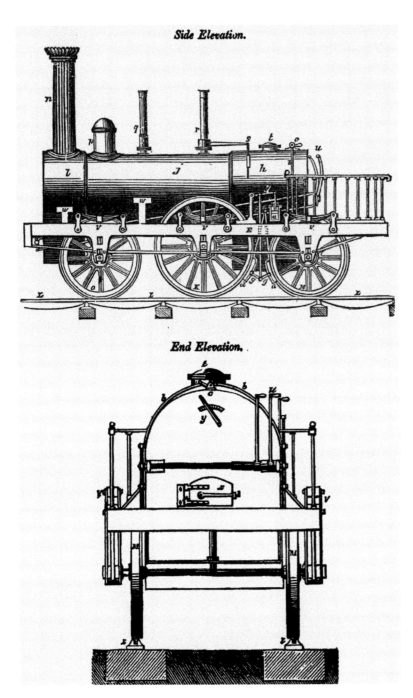

Side Elevation.

End Elevation.

Details from Robert Stephenson's patent application of 1833; note the steam-brake prominently mounted on the firebox.

she exploded while working a goods train up the Whiston Incline, killing both of her crew. Despite this tragedy, she was rebuilt and put back into service.

Just as it had been a logical evolution from 2-2-0 Planet type to the 2-2-2 Patentee, so too the evolution from the 0-4-0 Samson to the 0-4-2 'Large Samson' class, of which *Lion* is a member.

The first locomotive to run in Germany was *Der Adler,* a Patentee built in 1835 for the Nuremberg-Furth Railway. This replica was built in 1935.

Le Belge was the first locomotive in Belgium. She was built in 1835 by John Cockerill at his works in Seraing, near Liège, Belgium. This wooden replica was built in 1885.

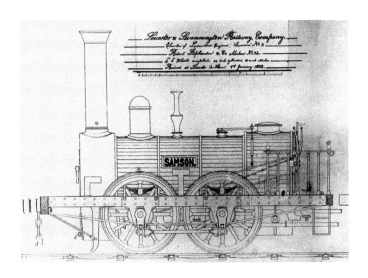

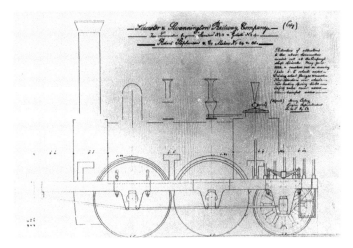

Evolution of the Large Samson class: take an 0-4-0 Samson (top); add a frame extension to support the carrying wheels (centre); and create an 0-4-2 Large Samson luggage engine (bottom).

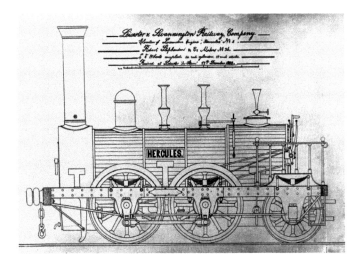

John Melling

John Melling (1781–1856) had been appointed 'Foreman of the Repairing Shops' at the Brickfield station, near Edgehill in Liverpool, on the Liverpool & Manchester Railway in 1833, having worked for the L&M from the very beginning; his colleague at the opposite end of the line in Manchester was Alexander Fyfe (c. 1790–1848). Melling's son Thomas (1817–96) worked as his assistant until 1837 when he moved to join the Grand Junction Railway as their Superintendent. John Melling was of an inventive turn of mind and presented several of his ideas to the Board of Directors for their perusal, including a firebox with hollow, water-filled fire bars with a water tank underneath acting as a feed water heater (1832); a hollow double axle (1833) which allowed one wheel to rotate at a different speed to aid locomotives going around curves; and a steam-operated 'coupling wheel' (1833) which could be raised or lowered between the driving and carrying wheels of a locomotive to increase its adhesion. The Directors saw promise in these ideas and granted full-scale trials with his firebox and 'coupling wheel' ideas.

In 1837 locomotive repair and maintenance was united at Brickfield Yard, and the sheds at Ordsall Lane in Manchester were scaled down. Thus, John Melling found himself in overall charge of the locomotive shop and able to give free reign to his ideas, for which he received letters patent in October 1837. Melling's Patent Application (No. 7410 of 26 July 1837) included six different inventions. The first was his 'Coupling Wheel', which did away with the need for outside coupling rods, and helped increase adhesion with a heavy load or when rails were 'in a wet or greasy state'. A third, smaller wheel, which could be raised or lowered via a steam cylinder, was placed between the driving and leading wheel. In its lowered position, it coupled both wheels together. This did away with the need for coupling rods, but also meant additional adhesion was available when required through the coupling of extra wheels. Melling noted that:

A contemporary French depiction of the Stephenson-type luggage engine, alias 'Large Samson'.

The contrivance is very advantageous in comparison with the ordinary previous mode of coupling between any two wheels, because, if the rail be dry or the adhesion sufficient, the anti-friction wheel may be lifted off and remain idle, while the ordinary system of outside cranks and connecting rods must always continue working, and thus, at certain times, act as an incumbrance. Another important feature ... is the smoothness with which the engine works ... compared to engines coupled in the ordinary manner. The improvement is effected by transmitting a considerable portion of the weight from the cranked or driving axle to the straight or independent axle, which entirely prevents the tremulous lateral motion of ordinary locomotive engines. (*Repertory of Patent Inventions*, 1838: 2–3)

The wheels could thus be coupled or uncoupled at will, and 'at any rate of running'. The first locomotive to be so fitted was *Firefly* in February 1837, and *Arrow* was so fitted in May 1837. Although seemingly 'Heath Robinson', Melling's coupling wheel was revived by Francis Webb, Chief Mechanical Engineer of the LNWR, in the 1880s.

Melling's second invention was similar: a brake which used two small wheels that could be raised or lowered by steam between the driving wheel and another wheel-set. As the two small wheels ran in opposite directions, a braking effect was produced. His third invention was using hollow water-filled firebars and a method of heating the feed water by placing a water tank underneath the firebars: 'The falling cinders from the furnace, as they are caught by this water ash-box, will heat the water therein.' The water from this tank was able to circulate with that in the tender tank via leather hoses, meaning that the tender water would be heated. Waste steam from the safety valve could also be turned via a special cock into the tender tank, helping to heat the feed-water in the tank under the firebox. A fifth was to use a steam jet 'for the purpose of cleansing the rails from snow, grease, or sand...'

His most successful innovation was his radial valve gear, the Grand Junction engine *Lynx* being the first so equipped in October 1837. It was then adopted by the L&M in March 1838. Instead of using eccentrics to drive the valves, Melling derived it from a pin in the centre of the connecting rod working in a slotted link:

Mr Melling ... made a stud fast in the middle of the connecting rod, which by the nature of the connecting-rod motion, described a species of elliptical curve ... The stud worked in a slot formed in a lever, of which this axis was placed in the centre of the oval. This arm the pin carried round with it, and on the same axis a small crank worked the valve-rod, like an ordinary eccentric. (Clark 1855: 23)

The 'small cranks' worked four gab-ended connecting rods, which, via a single lever on the footplate, could be simultaneously raised or lowered to engage or disengage with a pin on a rocker arm, providing fore or back-gear. A list of locomotives drawn up by Melling dated 10 April 1839 shows that some thirteen locomotives of the L&M fleet were fitted with his patent valve gear (*Lion* among them). The remaining L&M locomotives all used the 'old hand eccentric gear' as used on *Planet*.

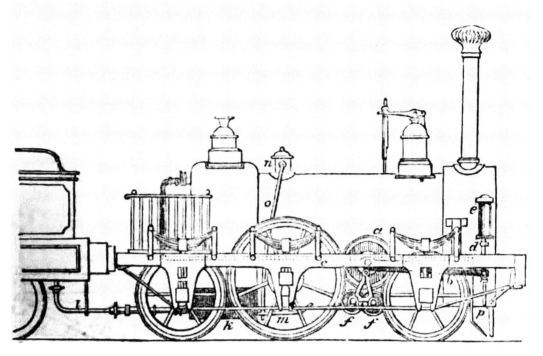

John Melling's patent application of 1837 included several different 'improvements': prominent are the patent coupling wheel (a) and brake (ff), raised and lowered by cylinder (e).

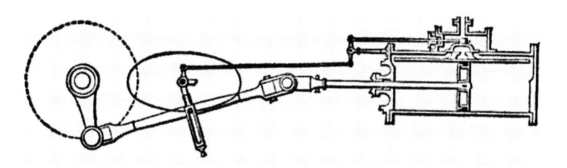

John Melling's patent radial valve gear, which was originally fitted to *Lion* and her sisters. The drive for the valves is derived from a stud fixed to the middle of the connecting rod. Unfortunately, the resulting valve timing was a little 'lumpy'.

Legal Trouble

At the recommendation of John Melling, the L&M Directors ordered ten locomotives in October 1837, and a further four in spring 1838 in order to handle the expected increase in traffic. They were to be fitted with Melling's patent improvements. *Lion* and her sisters were ordered on 2 October 1837:

The treasurer stated that in conformity with the instructions of the Board he had contracted for Ten Locomotive Engines, viz. With Todd, Kitson & Laird of Leeds, for -

2 Luggage engines with 11-inch cylinder, 20 inch stroke to be delivered on the 30th April 1838 £1,100 each.

2 Coaching Engines with 11 ½ inch cylinder, 18 inch stroke. 5' 6' wheels. To be delivered on the 30th June for £1,060 each.

2 Bank Engines with 13-inch cylinder, 20 inch stroke, to be delivered 30th September 1838 for £1, 1130 each.

With Benjamin Hick of Bolton for -

2 Luggage engines. 11 inch cylinder, 20 inch stroke. To be delivered 30th June 1838 for £1,350 each.

With Rothwell & Co, for -

2Coaching Engines. 11 inch cylinders, 18 inch stroke.
> 1 to be delivered by the 31st May
> 1 to be delivered by the 30th June 1838 for £1,250 each. (RAIL371/10)

These engines would become *Lion, Tiger, Leopard, Panther, Elephant, Buffalo, Samson, Goliah, Rokeby* and *Roderick.*

Melling, however, got into trouble with the Board of the L&M: he had recommended that they adopt his various improvements for their new locomotives, but had failed to inform them not only that he had in fact patented them, but that he also expected a royalty payment! Suffice to say the L&M Board was not impressed when they found this out in December 1837. Melling was brought before the Board in January 1838 and severely reprimanded, and when the Board suggested he sign a legal agreement with them for the use of his patents, he refused. Eventually, Melling backed down and agreed that he would

Lion standing proudly on Water Street Bridge, Liverpool Road, in spring 2007. (David Boydell)

not charge royalties for as long as he was employed by the L&M. The Board made a gift of 100 guineas to cover any royalties for the eleven engines then being built, and Melling agreed he would only charge his employers half the fee for further use of his inventions. Finally, in March 1838 the L&M Board ruled that Melling would be paid 50 guineas for the use of his 'patent improvements' and that their locomotives were to be fitted with his patent valve gear, coupling wheel and feed-water heater as they came in for repair.

But this was not the end of the saga: Melling Senior and Junior had also attempted a similar ruse with the Directors of the Grand Junction. At the suggestion of Thomas Melling the GJR had ordered ten locomotives fitted with his father's patent improvements, but had also failed to inform them they were patented. The furious GJR Directors flatly refused to pay Melling's royalties of £52 per engine, and instead presented him with 200 guineas (twice what the L&M Directors had paid) for the ten engines built according to his patent.

In October 1838, the L&M issued written specifications for its locomotives. Boiler barrels were to be constructed from Low Moor iron, consisting of four narrow plates, each the full length of the barrel, with longitudinal joints, lap-jointed together. As a prelude to building their own locomotives, in 1839 the Directors ordered that locomotive wheels, axles, frame and valve gear were to be made 'in house' under the direction of Melling at Edge Hill and only the boilers and tubes be contracted for.

The Iron Lion

Lion was built by the Leeds firm of Todd, Kitson & Laird. The company had been formed on 1 September in a converted mill in Hunslet by James Kitson (1807–95) – who had been apprenticed to Fenton, Murray & Wood in Leeds and had latterly worked for Robert Stephenson & Co. – and Charles Todd – who had also been apprenticed to Fenton, Murray & Wood – with the money coming from David Laird, a prosperous yeoman farmer. Thus the company had only been in existence for a month when they received their lucrative contract from the L&M. But the partnership was only short-lived, being dissolved in April 1839 almost as soon as the last engine for the L&M had been delivered. Todd joined forces with another Leeds engineer, John Shepherd (1795–1852), yet another apprentice from Fenton, Murray & Wood, as 'Shepherd & Todd' while Kitson formed a partnership with Laird.

Lion was the first locomotive to be delivered, at a cost of £1,100, in summer 1838. The *Leeds Times* of Saturday 4 August 1838 announced:

Messrs Todd, Kitson & Laird, of this town, have just completed their first locomotive engine manufactured for the Liverpool & Manchester Railway. The engine was exhibited to a number of respectable gentlemen on Tuesday last, who spoke in the most flattering terms of the excellence of its manufacture.

The *Leeds Mercury* of the same date added:

New Loco-Motive Engine. We witnessed the trial on Monday last of a new and very powerful locomotive engine, built by Messrs. Todd, Kitson & Laird of this town, for the Manchester and Liverpool Railway. Benjamin Gott esq. and T. B. Pease esq., and several other gentlemen connected with railways in this neighbourhood, were present, and expressed, in the highest terms, their admiration the excellent workmanship and appearance of the engine 'The Lion'.

Lion and *Tiger* were used as 'bank or help-up engines' on the Whiston and Sutton Incline Planes. The *Manchester Courier* announced in November 1838:

New and Powerful Locomotive Engine, built by Messrs. Todd, Kitson & Laird of Leeds, has been placed on the railway, to work as a 'help-up' Engine on the Whiston Incline Plane, where it is hoped it will do the work of two Engines. It is shortly to be joined by a second Locomotive of the similar type.

While employed as the Whiston banker, *Lion* was involved in the tragic explosion of *Patentee* on Monday 12 November 1838. *Patentee* was the pilot engine coupled to *Fury* (the train engine) at the head of a heavy train of forty-three loaded goods wagons (probably weighing 250 tons), assisted from the rear by the newly arrived *Lion*, driven by Joseph Greenall. Greenall was a Leeds lad and had probably arrived with *Lion* as a fitter from Todd, Kitson & Laird. While toiling up the incline, *Patentee* blew up with an explosion 'which is stated to have resembled the firing of a cannon [and] was heard at Prescot and other places, more than a mile distant'. According to the *Manchester Courier* (17 November 1838), 'the Engine was shattered to pieces, and the tubes were totally destroyed'. The Engineman, Charles Warburton, was found:

Forty yards distant ... his right leg was broken, and his head terribly mangled ... The Fireman ... Samuel Jones, a lad of not more than eighteen years of age ... was found in the opposite direction. His left leg was literally severed from his body, and lay two yards distant from it.

At the inquest, John Melling was called as witness and could not account for the explosion: the lead plug had not melted, suggesting the water level had not dropped dangerously low; the boiler plates were found to have been sound; and he dismissed the idea that the crew had tampered with the safety valves as 'Warburton was an old and experienced engineer'.

Warburton had, as per regulation, wanted to divide the train to run it up the bank, but had been persuaded not to by Greenall. A verdict of accidental death was recorded and a deodand – a medieval custom of placing a fine on any property that had taken human life – of 20*s* was placed on *Patentee*. It is likely that the cause of the explosion was due to a fault inherent in the design as the drag-pin (where the tender connected to the locomotive) was riveted directly to the back of the firebox, rather than to the frames, so when under extreme load, as *Patentee* was, the firebox could be literally ripped apart. Following the explosion the Directors recommended that 'the staying of the Firebox above the Fire Door and Boiler End next the Chimney were strong', suggesting the cause of the explosion lay not with the boiler but the firebox, and the drag-pin being riveted to it. *Lion* was involved in a second accident on the Whiston Incline in 1840 when she derailed, breaking an axle and causing

Lion in steam in May 1980 at the Rocket 150 celebrations.

'much damage to the machinery'. Perhaps it was the crank axle which broke as the rivet pattern on *Lion*'s right-hand side driving wheel horn guide is different to that on the left.

With the delivery of the more powerful *Elephant* and *Buffalo* from Todd, Kitson & Laird in March 1839, *Lion* and *Tiger* were put on the more mundane duties of hauling goods trains. *Lion* probably had a tractive effort of 2,500 lbs, and is recorded in summer 1839 as regularly working 75-ton goods trains from Liverpool to Manchester and back, and being able to work them up the Whiston and Sutton inclines without any assistance. On a typical day, she was described as being in steam for over 16 hours, but was in fact only doing 7 hours of 'useful work' in making four full trips from Liverpool to Manchester (120 miles in total), during which time she burned 12 cwt 1 qr 8 lbs of coke, of which 2 cwt was going to waste keeping her in steam while she was standing idle. On average she burned 39 lbs of coke per mile, or about half a pound of coke per ton per mile. Despite being in steam for such a long period, her driver and fireman were only paid per trip made rather than the number of hours spent with their engine.

Rebuild and Standardisation

In September 1839, the L&M Directors were considering inviting an outside contractor to manage their locomotive department. Henry Booth, the General Superintendent, was empowered to reorganise the locomotive department. In November he gave Melling three months' notice to quit. All mechanical work was to be centralised at Edge Hill, which was to be considerably expanded. Edward Woods (1814–1903) was to assume responsibility of the Engineering Department (which included locomotives) while John Dewrance (1803–61) from Messrs Peel, Williams & Peel of Manchester was appointed as Locomotive Superintendent and Foreman of the Engine Shops. The L&M bought 10,000 square yards of land at Wavertree Lane in order to expand their works.

John Dewrance was faced with a rather motley collection of locomotives. Following practical experiments made with valves and valve gears (1838–41), Woods decided to adopt long-travel long-lap valves as standard in his locomotive fleet, together with standard cylinders and valve gear. He thus resolved to build new locomotives and to rebuild existing locomotives as a stop-gap. He reported to the Chairman in 1841 that locomotive construction had commenced at Edgehill and the locomotive fleet had been organised into three categories:

1. The 'New' Engines are those which have been built entirely by the Company, and, which from the uniformity observed in their construction, rank *first* in value.
2. The 'Rebuilt' Engines are such of the old Engines as have had all their parts renewed with the exception perhaps of the boiler, firebox and framing, and rank *second* in value.
3. The 'Repaired' Engines are such of the old Engines have undergone thorough repair without altering the cylinders, gearing etc. to conform with the most approved models, and rank *third* in value.

Lion and the other 'Melling Patents' came under the second category, faced with relatively new but non-standard engines, with peculiar valve gear and boilers for which royalty payments were now liable. The totality of these rebuilds is shown by the fact they cost around £800, while one of Dewrance's new Bird-class cost only £650, creating virtually (or entirely?) new locomotives in all but name.

Lion's original boiler was of the 'long plate' type, made from four longitudinal iron plates, lap-riveted together. It was therefore slightly oval in cross-section (3 feet 6 inches x 3 feet 3 inches), 7 feet 4 inches long with 126 tubes of 1¾ inches outside diameter,

Lion's footplate. Her controls are incredibly simple, consisting of a single sight-glass, twin Salter safety valves acting as a pressure gauge, regulator and reversing lever (which you pull back to go forward).

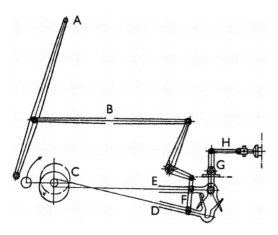

Above and right: When *Lion* was rebuilt by John Dewrance, the opportunity was taken to fit her with new cylinders, valves and valve gear – in this case the opposed-gab valve gear developed by Buddicom.

providing a heating surface of 450 square feet, to which the firebox added a further 30 square feet. Her cylinders were 11 x 20 inches. The present boiler on *Lion* was built by the Mersey Docks & Harbour Board in 1865, perhaps using an earlier boiler as a pattern. This boiler, with its high-crowned wagon-top firebox, is made from Low Moor iron, and is 8 feet 6 inches long and 3 feet 3 inches in diameter (over a foot longer than the original). It has ninety-eight 2-inch outside diameter tubes, and the firebox is just shy of 40 inches square. New cylinders 13 x 20 inches were fitted at Edgehill, but her present cylinders measure 14 x 18 inches and must date post-1845 as Edward Woods did not list any locomotives with cylinders of those dimensions to the Gauge Commissioners.

Although thought by Warren (1930) and Jarvis & Morris (1980) to date from 1838, the present valve gear on *Lion* dates from her major rebuild at Edgehill, when John Dewrance replaced Melling's patent radial valve gear with that developed by William Barber Buddicom (Chapter 2) in 1840 for the Grand Junction Railway. Buddicom used four fixed eccentrics on the crank axle. The eccentric rods terminated with opposed V-hooks, which can be engaged on a pin working a rocking shaft that in turn drives the valve spindles. This valve gear has a few idiosyncrasies: in order to engage fore-gear, the reversing lever has to be pulled backwards. Apprentices at Ruston Diesels Ltd (where *Lion* was restored to steam in 1979) found that it was impossible to change gear when *Lion* was stationary and that this could only be achieved while the locomotive was coasting, with the steam shut off. This also meant that *Lion* could be driven like her predecessors, using back-pressure in the cylinders as a brake to bring the locomotive to a stand. Alan Middleton, who drove her in 1980 at the 'Great Railway Exhibition' held at Liverpool Road station, Manchester, remembered:

She was very docile, but a bit idiosyncratic. If you wanted to put her in forward gear, you had to pull the great heavy lever backwards... There was no brakes, so to slow her down you had to put her in reverse... She used very little coal, just a few rounds now and then. The problem was stopping her blowing off. It was never a problem to light up without a blower. It was run seven days a week and never got cold and so would always draw. She'd do anything you asked of her. She's smaller than *Furness 20* but had extra wheels under the cab. It'd run like the clappers on the straight and level but it took time to get there.

Lion has driving wheels 5 feet in diameter at 6-foot centres; the trailing wheels are 3 feet 6 inches in diameter, giving an overall wheelbase of 12 feet. With her present boiler, she weighs 18 tons 7 cwt in working order. Ludicrously small clearances on *Lion* are evidence of the major rebuild in the 1840s: the wheels run extremely close to the smokebox; the clamping plates on the axle springs on the inner plate frames have been chamfered on one side to prevent them being struck by the balance web on the crank axle as it rotates; the modern (1929) boiler cladding has been worn away by the crank throws.

John and Thomas Melling later established Rainhill Iron Works as 'Melling & Son, engineers, millwrights, iron & brass founders, boiler makers'. They built three locomotives for the Grand Junction Railway (1841–42) and patented a combined atmospheric and high-pressure steam engine (1846); railway wheels (1847); and an iron-bar twisting machine (1848).

Of *Lion*'s sisters, *Tiger* was scrapped in 1850; *Elephant* was scrapped in 1847; and *Buffalo* soldiered on until sold out of service to a railway in Bulgaria in 1867. *Lion* was sold to the Mersey Docks & Harbour Board in May 1859 for £400. She was re-boilered in 1865 at a cost of £300 and worked the Liverpool docks until 1873, when she was used to power a pump at Princes Dock. *Lion* was discovered in the pump house in 1922 and was purchased by members of the Liverpool Engineering Society in 1927. She was restored to running order for the Railway Centenary of 1930 at the Crewe Works of the LMS, and thanks to Sir Henry Fowler (Chief Mechanical Engineer of the LMS), largely as a gesture of goodwill. *Lion*'s career in preservation has seen her steamed for the film *Victoria the Great* (1937); make an

Lion as she was when recovered from a pump house on Liverpool Docks in 1927. Her carrying wheels were luckily discovered lurking in the pump house.

Above: *Lion* was restored by the LMS at Crewe between 1929 and 1930. One of the most controversial decisions was the fitting of the unauthentic large brass cover over the firebox. Part of the 'restoration' included building a new tender using parts from a scrapped Furness Railway example.

Right: *Lion* went on a UK-wide tour between 1980 and 1983. She is seen here at Keighley in summer 1981.

appearance at the centenary celebrations of the London & Birmingham Railway at Euston (1938); the George Stephenson Centenary at Chesterfield (1948); and in the film *The Lady with the Lamp* (1951). But it was with the 1953 Ealing comedy *The Titfield Thunderbolt* that *Lion* came to international stardom, and is perhaps best remembered.

CHAPTER 4

Broad Gauge Interlude

Robert Stephenson's six-wheel Patentee type was built in considerable numbers both at home and abroad between 1834 and 1840 – so much so they became the basis of the 2-2-2 passenger and 0-4-2 goods locomotive for the next forty or so years. The six-wheel locomotive also appeared as a 2-4-0 (two being built for the Leeds & Selby Railway by Fenton, Murray & Jackson, and also finding particular favour in France) and as the heavyweight 0-6-0 *Atlas* on the Leicester & Swannington Railway. Delivered in 1834 she was the then-largest locomotive, weighing in at 17 tons: her boiler was 8 feet 6 inches long, 3 feet 11½ inches in diameter with 154 iron tubes that were 1⅝ inches in diameter. This generated steam for 16 x 20-inch cylinders; driving wheels were 4 feet 6 inches in diameter, delivering 60 hp. She was the prototype for the six-coupled goods engine that would be built in vast numbers – as both a tender and tank locomotive – for the next 130 years.

Thus, by the late 1830s the Stephenson Patentee type six-wheel locomotive had virtually become the standard passenger and goods locomotive. Just as it had been natural to add an extra axle to the earlier four-wheel Planet types, so it was a natural evolution that they would be built for different gauges, too.

AN EARLY GREAT WESTERN BROAD GAUGE ENGINE 'VULCAN'.

Vulcan (Charles Tayleur & Co.) was the first locomotive to run on Brunel's broad gauge on 28 December 1837. She was rebuilt as a tank engine in 1846 and withdrawn in 1868.

It was to Robert Stephenson & Co. that Daniel Gooch (1816–89) turned in desperation to find locomotives for the fledgling Great Western Railway. This should not be surprising, given that Gooch had been a draughtsman at Forth Street, where he had designed two 6-foot-gauge locomotives for Russia, and had previously worked in the erecting shop at the Vulcan Foundry of Charles Tayleur & Co. (a joint concern between Robert Stephenson and Charles Tayleur). Gooch had been presented with 'the most extraordinary collection of freaks' in order to operate the railway, a result of peculiar design parameters set out by Brunel. Of the ten locomotives, the only successful early engines were the two Stephenson-built locomotives, *North Star* and *Morning Star*. Originally built for the New Orleans Railway to 5 feet 6 inches gauge, *North Star* was purchased by Gooch and altered to 7-foot gauge. In *North Star*, the diameter of the driving wheels was increased to 7 feet but *Morning Star* retained her original 6-foot 6-inch driving wheels and worked the first passenger train out of Paddington on 4 June 1838. *North Star* was a 2-2-2 Patentee type with 7-foot diameter driving wheels and cylinders of 16 x 16 inches. The boiler was 8 feet 6 inches long and 4 feet in diameter with 167 tubes. The valves were worked by four fixed eccentrics and gab gear, with upward-facing gabs as on *Patentee*. The crank axle was supported via outside sandwich frames and four intermediate iron plate frames, in the Stephenson manner. *Morning Star* was similar, but with driving wheels that were 6 inches smaller. Of these two locomotives Brunel wrote: 'We have a splendid engine of Stephenson's, it would be a beautiful ornament in the most elegant drawing room.'

Nicholas Wood reported the opening of the Great Western in June 1838: 'The engine employed on this occasion was ... the 'North Star,' to which was attached a train of carriages containing nearly 200 passengers; with this train the engine performed a journey in 47 minutes the distance being 22½ miles, which is at the rate of 28 miles an hour.' She is recorded as achieving a sped of 45 mph with a gross load (including engine and tender) of 50 tons and 30 mph with a 110-ton load.

North Star was heavily rebuilt in 1854 (after being put on secondary duties) at Swindon Works with a new domeless boiler, new cylinders and a longer wheelbase. Her original Stephenson pattern 'gas pipe' wheels were retained; the amount of material dating from

A Victorian postcard of *North Star* (1837) as she was at the end of her working life in 1870. She had been rebuilt with a new, domeless, boiler in 1854 and was tragically scrapped in 1906.

1837 was probably minimal. She was finally withdrawn in 1871 after a working life of thirty-three years and having run 429,000 miles. She was initially preserved at Swindon Works, but was tragically scrapped in 1905 on the orders of G. J. Churchward (1857–1933). A full-size (non-working) replica was built in 1925, incorporating some original parts such as the crank axle and driving wheels, as well as other components that had been saved.

Robert Stephenson & Co. supplied ten other locomotives to the same design between 1839 and 1841: 7-foot driving wheels and cylinders 15 x 18 inches for the first eight locomotives and 15½ x 19 inches for the final pair. Gooch was given permission to build his own locomotives in 1840, and he took as his prototype the successful Stephenson Star class. In order to build his locomotives, Gooch established the famous Swindon Works in 1841:

> The whole of the locomotive department of the Great Western Railway, hitherto at Wootton road, has been removed to the Swindon Station, thus enhancing the importance of the town, to which the immense range of buildings already completed, and those now in progress, give an imposing appearance. A great number of houses are to be built in the ensuing year Swindon. (*Salisbury and Winchester Journal*, 29 November 1841)

Gooch's personal assistant was Richard Peacock (1820–89), formerly Locomotive Superintendent of the Leeds & Selby Railway, who after a fruitful career with the Manchester, Sheffield & Lincolnshire Railway went on to form Beyer, Peacock in 1854. Despite initially having a difficult relationship with Brunel, Archibald Sturrock (1816–1909) was appointed Works Manager at Swindon, leaving in 1850 to join the Great Northern Railway. Gooch set down strict design specifications (including materials), to ensure standardisation and interchangeability of parts. Some sixty-two members of the Firefly class were delivered between March 1840 and 1842, with twenty coming from Fenton, Murray & Jackson of Leeds, while the titular member of the class, *Firefly*, was built by Jones, Tuner & Evans of the Viaduct Foundry, Newton-Le-Willows.

A Victorian photograph of the titular *Firefly* built by Jones, Turner & Evans of Newton-le-Willows in 1840.

The Fireflys had 15 x 18-inch cylinders with 7-foot diameter driving wheels and 4-foot diameter carrying wheels. While Gooch's boilers were little larger than those on the standard gauge, only 4 feet diameter (compared to the 3 feet 6 inches of *Patentee*) and 8 feet 6 inches long (compared to the 7 feet 6 inches of *Patentee*), his fireboxes were almost the full width of the outside frames. The firebox shell was high-crowned, forming a vault or 'Gothic arch' and creating a large steam space above the hottest part of the boiler where the most steam was generated, similar to the fireboxes of Edward Bury (Chapter 5). On her first recorded run, *Firefly* attained a maximum speed of 58 mph – far higher than any contemporary narrow gauge Stephenson locomotive. It was a member of the class, *Phlegethon*, which pulled the first Royal Train on 13 June 1842. The class had a service life of twenty-five to thirty years, the last example being withdrawn in 1879. Another Leeds-built Firefly, *Ixion*, took part in the famous gauge trials of 1846.

A working replica of *Firefly* was built by the Firefly Trust and first steamed in 2005. She is seen here at the Didcot Railway Centre.

Firefly, together with *Iron Duke* and replica broad gauge carriages, are on display at the Didcot Railway Centre in the Transfer Shed, at the end of a short section of broad gauge running line.

Detail of *Firefly*'s driving wheel and nameplate.

Above left: *Firefly*'s impressive 'Arc de Cloitre' (alias 'Gothick') firebox. Prominent are the row of three test-cocks to ascertain water level in the boiler and the reversing lever operating the gab valve gear.

Above right: The historic 1850s Didcot Transfer Shed at the Didcot Railway Centre, which was used to tranship goods from the broad to standard gauge. The track here is dual gauge, and the width of Brunel's broad gauge is readily apparent.

Gooch's next essay in locomotive design was *Great Western,* the prototype of his famous *Iron Duke* class. With her 8-foot driving wheels, the *London Evening Chronicle* described her as 'the biggest of its race in the world' when relaying an experiment made with her running from London to Bristol in a record-breaking time of 2 hours and 24 minutes. The *Taunton Courier* gushed:

> TRIUMPH OF THE LOCOMOTIVE. A great sensation has been created in the engineering world, the arrival at Exeter of a mammoth locomotive engine, called The Great Western. She was built from the designs of D. Gooch, Esq., the Superintendent-chief of the locomotive department the Great Western Railway at the Swindon works, which are the most extensive and perfect works on any line of Railway in the kingdom. The manager of the works is A. Sturrock, Esq., and most ably has he executed the designs of the chief. Her weight is 28 tons; she has 1900 square feet heating surface, of which 160 is firebox; cylinders 18 inches in diameter, strokes 24 inches; driving wheels 8 feet in diameter; supporting wheels four feet 6 inches. This engine, when doing equal work with smaller engines, consumes less fuel. But staking her vast proportions, she baffles all previous conjecture by the results of her speed. She came down to Exeter with the Express Train on Monday last, the short space of 3 hours and 28 minutes, actual time of running—the maximum speed for several miles being at the rate of 59½ miles per hour. (*Taunton Courier and Western Advertiser,* 10 June 1846)

Great Western incorporated several novel features, including direct drive for the valves and two regulators, one per cylinder:

> The arrangement of the working parts is much simplified in this powerful engine, by the valve working laterally on the port face of the cylinder, giving a level line from centre of the crank axle to the valve and spindle which causes a direct action, and does away with motion bars or rocking shafts. There are regulator valves one for each engine, which is the greatest advantage in case one of the engines failing, by the security which it affords when one engine is disconnected. The wheels are the most perfect piece of forging that can be imagined. The large driving wheels look very light, all the parts being composed of wrought iron. The spokes are all welded together at the centre, which forms light and strong wrought iron nave. The additional heating surface of the engine abridges the time necessary to get her ready, it takes about one hour and three quarters to get up steam with cold water. She adds another laurel to the mechanical honours achieved by the Scientific Chief of the locomotive department. Mr Gooch's patent for applying the steel tire to the locomotive wheel was a vast improvement, inasmuch promoted durability, and consequent accuracy of form in the wheel, by which the curve is preserved, and security promoted. (*Taunton Courier and Western Advertiser,* 10 June 1846)

Following in quick succession was *Iron Duke,* delivered in April 1847 as the first eight-wheeled locomotive with a 2+2-2-2 wheel arrangement; the additional pair of leading carrying wheels being provided following *Great Western's* leading wheel set breaking under stress. The massive outside sandwich frames were cranked over the driving axle bearings, to accommodate the large size of the driving wheels. There were also two inner iron plate frames and a centre stay, in the Stephenson tradition. The valves were worked using Gooch's stationary link valve gear, which was a modified form of the Stephenson-Howe link motion. Gooch took the opportunity to raise boiler pressure to 100 psi, and together with cylinders measuring 18 x 24 inches the loco had a nominal tractive effort of 8,000 lbs – four times that of *Lion*, clearly demonstrating not only the speed of locomotive development, but the advantages of the broad gauge. Under trials, *Iron Duke* achieved an average speed of 53.4 mph with a load of 105 tons (including locomotive and tender), but the highest recorded speed was 78.2 mph! The *London Evening Standard* described *Iron Duke* as 'extraordinary':

A full-size working replica of *Iron Duke* was built for the 150th anniversary of the opening of the Great Western Railway in 1988.

The *Iron Duke* replica on display at the National Railway Museum at York in 1988.

Originally named *Charles Russell* after a GWR director, *Lord of the Isles* was built in 1851 and displayed at the Great Exhibition. She was withdrawn in 1884, and was tragically scrapped as recently as 1906.

> The 'Iron Duke' ... took one of the express trains from London to Swindon, a distance of 77 miles, in 71 minutes, and from Swindon to London in 70 minutes, stopping at Didcot both times. The maximum velocity is said to have been nearly 80 miles an hour, maintaining for 8 miles together a rate of 75 miles [an hour], and averaging ... a rate of 66 miles an hour, an unrivalled performance ... The steadiness of the engine at these high velocities surprised even those accustomed to other Broad Gauge engines ... Who, then, can doubt the competing gauge can readily and safely maintain a rate of 50 miles an hour ... when the 'Iron Duke' class are all completed? (*London Evening Standard*, 14 June 1847)

Twenty-nine members of the Iron Duke class were built between 1847 and 1855, the last built member of the class being the aptly named *Sebastopol*. The last member of the class in service, *Lord of the Isles,* built in 1851 and originally named *Charles Russell*, was preserved at Swindon in 1884, but together with *North Star* it was ignominiously cut up in 1905.

Working Replicas

Although the last of the broad gauge was taken up in 1892, two working broad gauge replicas have been built which convey something of the size and majesty of Brunel's Great Western. The first, *Iron Duke,* was built in anticipation of the 150th anniversary of the Great Western Railway, incorporating the boiler, cylinders, crank axle, valve gear and inside frames from a 'J-94' tank engine. As a result several design compromises had to be made; the boiler, for example, is 6 inches smaller in diameter than the original (4 feet 3 inches compared to 4 feet 9¾ inches), but by mounting the boiler higher, the original boiler top line was maintained, and usefully also allowed space for the larger than original crank throws. The original crank axle was cut and lengthened to suit the broad gauge and new wheels were fabricated. *Iron Duke* first steamed in Hyde Park, on a length of specially laid track. She was regularly steamed at the National Railway Museum, York, together with two replica carriages. *Iron Duke* visited Bristol to take part in the Brunel 200 celebrations, and since 2013 she has been on static display at the Didcot Railway Centre. Replica broad gauge carriages were also built.

A replica of *Firefly* was built by the Firefly Trust (established 1982), taking over twenty years to be completed. The boiler, built by Israel Newton & Sons, was first steamed in October 2002 and the rolling chassis turned over under air in the December of the same year. *Firefly* entered traffic at the Great Western Society's base at Didcot on 3 April 2005, running on a short stretch of broad gauge demonstration line. In 2013 she was gifted to the Great Western Society. Rather like the replica *Planet*, *Firefly* was built to conform with modern safety standards, including injectors and an air brake (a lesson learned from *Planet,* which has air brakes that have to be charged from a compressor) so she can work passenger trains. With his Firefly class, Gooch had developed what was to be the standard Great Western express locomotive until the end of the broad gauge. In doing so, they maintained outside sandwich frames and other features of the classic Stephenson locomotive until the 1890s.

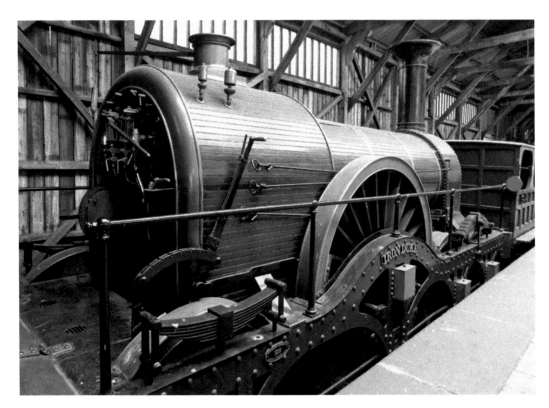

The *Iron Duke* replica dwarfs *Firefly,* and makes the replica of *Planet* look like a toy! It's hard to tell the replica was built from an Austerity saddle tank.

Iron Duke's enormous 8-foot diameter driving wheels and nameplate.

Iron Duke's cab layout, showing some of its 'Austerity' provenance. The forward view is very restricted.

Replica broad gauge second-class carriage. (Gareth C. Price)

The Great Western were reluctant to carry third-class passengers, as shown by the crude open carriages they were carried in. (Gareth C. Price)

The 1925-built replica of *North Star* on display at Wavertree to mark the 'Railway Centenary' of 1930. She is seen here in company with *Columbine* of 1845.

Chapter 5

Copper Nobs and Bar Frames

Standing in the Great Hall of the National Railway Museum in York is *Coppernob*. Built for the Furness Railway at the Clarence Foundry, Liverpool, by Bury, Curtis & Kennedy in 1846, it had a working life of fifty-two years. She is a rare survivor of a type of locomotive which challenged the monopoly on locomotive design established by Robert Stephenson. Bury's locomotive designs used lightweight bar frames and D-plan fireboxes surmounted by a large, copper-clad steam dome. Bury is seldom considered in the history of locomotive development, but for more than a decade his locomotives were serious rivals to those of Stephenson. Although finding little favour in Britain and France, the key features of the Bury locomotive were popular in the United States and formed the basis of the nineteenth-century American locomotive.

Edward Bury was born in Salford and educated in Chester. His father was a timber merchant, and Edward was a partner in Gregson & Bury's Steam Saw Mill at Toxteth near Liverpool in 1823. He then entered into partnership with the Scottish engineer

'Th'owd Copper Nob': Furness Railway No. 3 of 1846. (Ian Hardman)

Coppernob on display in the Great Hall at the National Railway Museum, York. (Ian Hardman)

James Kennedy (1797–1886), who was a marine engineer by profession; Kennedy had, reputedly, been works manager at Robert Stephenson & Co. for sixteen months between 1824 and 1825, supervising the construction of the first locomotives for the Stockton & Darlington Railway. Subsequently he was appointed works manager of Mather, Dixon & Co. of Liverpool in December 1825, where he met Bury. The two went on to form

Detail of *Coppernob*'s number plate. (Douglas Roberts)

the partnership of Edward Bury & Co. in 1826, which became Bury, Curtis & Kennedy from 1842. Kennedy left the partnership in 1859. Based at the Clarence Foundry, Liverpool, Bury, Curtis & Kennedy built steam engines for mills, ships and locomotives. Unlike George Stephenson, Bury was an establishment figure, being an Anglican (with all the legal privileges that gave him), a member of the Institute of Civil Engineers (March 1830) and one of only two locomotive engineers to be a Fellow of the Royal Society (1844) – the other being Sir William Stanier. It is little wonder the two didn't see eye to eye: Bury was exactly the sort of 'establishment expert' who would raise Stephenson's hackles.

Th'owd *Coppernob*

Furness Railway No. 3 *Coppernob* was one of four locomotives delivered to the Furness Railway by Bury, Curtis & Kennedy between 1844 and 1846. A further eight to the same design were later supplied by William Fairbairn of Manchester from 1854 to 1861. *Coppernob* worked until 1897 and No. 4 until January 1898. The *Railway Magazine* remarked in 1899:

> For a long time this engine was the oldest at work in the world. Known as 'Old Copper Knob', it has been of great interest to many who have seen it working daily on the docks at Barrow-in-Furness ... [It] has been at work for nearly fifty-three years. The preservation of it as a monument is worthy of consideration. (*Railway Magazine*, Vol. IV: 217)

Coppernob and her sister were delivered by sea from Liverpool to Barrow, but according to W. F. Fancey, writing in the *Railway Magazine*:

> Barrow at this time was not possessed of power for lifting them out of the ship, consequently sheer-legs were erected, and, after several mishaps, No. 3 was landed on the beach, thence on plates and temporary lines to the nearest part of the mainline, on which

she was taken to the sheds, where all the motion and gearing were put together. (*Railway Magazine*, Vol. IV; 218)

The *Railway Magazine* couldn't estimate her total mileage as 'previous to 1857 it was not kept', but suggested 'there can be no doubt it will amount to a very high figure'. It also noted that the axles had 'been renewed three or four times', but the 'original framing, wheel-centres, and slide-bars still remain'. Whether the boiler and firebox date from 1846 or are a later replacement is not known, but clearly *Coppernob* contains a significant amount of material from her build date.

When she was photographed in 1899, *Coppernob* was the oldest working locomotive in the UK.

Coppernob was on display at Barrow-in-Furness station until 1941, when she suffered bomb damage. She was moved to Crewe Works for safekeeping. She is seen here prepared for transport (and minus chimney) opposite Dalton Tannery at Barrow.

Above and Right: *Coppernob* was stored at Horwich Works between 1946 and 1962, when she was put on display at the Clapham Railway Museum.

Dreadnought and *Liverpool*

Bury & Co.'s first locomotive was built in 1828 and named *Dreadnought*. She was going to be entered in the Rainhill Trials but was not complete in time. Of this locomotive Kennedy said:

> It had two inclined cylinders working down to cranks on a shaft carried across beneath the boiler, on which the shaft wheel for pitched chains was fixed, and this wheel gave motion to a pitched chain passing over pulleys on the fore and aft axles of the carriage, and so propelled the machine. This engine was formed with side rods working down to the cranks, the same way as the 'Locomotion.' The boiler was made with a fire tube and two return tubes. (*The Engineer*, 24 December 1875)

The description by Hardman Earle, one of the Liverpool & Manchester Directors, agrees with Kennedy, who notes both the chain drive and an 'accelerating wheel'. Mrs Bury wrote:

> She had the old plan of boiler and six wheels, with cylinders ten inches in diameter, two feet stroke, and two valves – one, the ordinary valve, the other the expansive valve – to allow the steam being worked expansively. (*Recollections*: 2)

Dreadnought was an 0-6-0 with inclined outside cylinders measuring 10 x 24 inches. Her driving wheels were 4 feet in diameter and she had a wheelbase of 8 feet 6 inches. Although missing Rainhill, *Dreadnought* was subsequently used during the construction of the Liverpool & Manchester Railway (1829–30). Her later history is somewhat confused: John Kennedy says she was sold to 'Mr Hargreaves of Bolton, and continued in use in traffic [on the Bolton & Leigh Railway] for twenty years'. Kennedy, however, might be mistaken,

Liverpool, the progenitor of the 'Bury' type locomotive with inside bar frames and D-shaped firebox, surmounted by a large copper cased steam dome. The large size of her 6-foot driving wheels is apparent.

having confused the later career of *Liverpool* (below) with that of *Dreadnought*. Ahrons (1923), however, suggests that 'Dreadnought was a complete failure', being too heavy for the lightly laid permanent way and frequently breaking crank pins on the drive-shaft, even after she had been rebuilt with lowered cylinders and better weight distribution. *The Engineer* (11 March 1898) adds:

> Dreadnought, being a six-coupled engine with outside cylinders, which, after trials on the Liverpool & Manchester Railway, was finally scrapped in December [1830] ... entailed a dead-loss to the company of £1500 between the cost of building and the price of the scrap.

Bury and Kennedy's second locomotive, built in 1830, was named *Liverpool*. She was an 0-4-0 with 6-foot diameter driving wheels and a return flue-boiler:

> This engine had a boiler like the Dreadnought, but the cylinders were horizontal, and the driving axle was cranked. A blowing cylinder was employed to provide the necessary draught, but as it made holes in the fire, it was discarded and a tubular boiler with a round firebox was substituted, with an exhausting jet in the chimney. (*The Engineer*, 24 December 1875)

Edward Woods (Engineer of the Liverpool & Manchester) described her in 1857:

> The 'Liverpool' was a four-wheeled coupled engine with cranked axles and cylinders under the smokebox. The hand-gearing was placed in front of the smoke-box, where the driver stood, the stoker being in the usual position, at the other extremity of the engine, or firebox end. The outer firebox was domed, and contained a very small internal firebox. The boiler was not multi-tubular ... but contained a number of convoluted [i.e. return] flues ... The furnace was urged by a blast from a pair of bellows working under the tender

and not by the aid of the blast-pipe ... In its first stage it did not resemble any form of engine now in use. (*Proceedings*: 24)

Kennedy suggested that *Liverpool* was the first locomotive to utilise horizontal cylinders under the smokebox and a cranked driving axle ('contrived and constructed by Mr Kennedy'), despite *Novelty* having used a cranked axle at the Rainhill Trials, and furthermore that Robert Stephenson had stolen the idea from the *Liverpool*:

'Liverpool' was started on the 22nd of July, 1830, by Mr Edward Bury ... The 'Planet' ... was not started until four and a half months afterwards ... The late Mr George Stephenson had told both Mr Bury and Mr Kennedy, after having seen the 'Liverpool' engine ... that his son, the present Robert Stephenson, had taken a fancy to the plan of the 'Liverpool' engine, and intended to make, immediately, a small engine on the same principle. (*Proceedings*: 22)

To this claim, Robert Stephenson replied:

'Planet' ... had been made ... and constructed under my direction, without any reference or knowledge of the 'Liverpool' ... Neither was there any analogy between the two machines, for the 'Planet' had a multi-tubular boiler, the fire being urged by a blast-pipe, and the cylinders, which were nearly as nearly horizontal as their position would permit, were fixed between the frames ... with the cylinders in the smokebox a cranked axle was indispensable, and there was not anything new in its use in locomotives. (*Proceedings*: 23)

Liverpool was rebuilt in 1831 with a new multi-tubular boiler with 131 tubes and had a round-topped D-plan iron inner firebox. Still fitted with 6-feet diameter wheels, *Liverpool* was involved in an accident in July 1831, after which it was fitted with smaller 4-foot 6-inch wheels. She established Bury's standard design practice:

- Wrought-iron bar frames.
- Inside bearings (two bearings per axle).
- D-plan, dome-topped inner firebox.
- Dome-topped outer firebox acting as a steam dome.

Bury & Co. built two 'standard' locomotives: the 'A' type 0-4-0 with coupled wheels for goods trains and the 2-2-0 'B' type for passenger working.

The Bury Locomotive

Liverpool had established the basic elements of the Bury design, a design which broke the mould from the Stephenson formula of outside sandwich frames, square fireboxes and six wheels. Bury's firebox design was similar to that of Braithwaite & Ericsson's *Novelty* of 1829: an upright, dome-topped cylinder containing a smaller cylinder for the firebox. It did not require any form of stay to support the inner firebox and the high dome of the outer firebox acted as an excellent steam collector. Many early Stephenson locomotives were prone to priming due to insufficient steam space, resulting in the fitting of larger and larger domes, or multiple domes. The 'gothic' firebox adopted by Stephenson in 1838 solved this problem in the same way as Braithwaite & Ericcson and Bury had done, by providing a large steam space over the hottest part of the boiler where the most steam was generated. However, the lack of stays for the inner firebox resulted in considerable controversy. George Stephenson, in his capacity as Engineer of the Liverpool & Manchester, thought the design was unsafe. Bury, in a paper presented to the Institute of Civil Engineers (of which George Stephenson was not a member) in March 1840, repudiated this claim:

> The firebox being cylindrical, with its back flattened so as to receive the tubes; its top, a sphere, with all the curves so as to enable the plates to resist the pressure of the steam ... without the ribs or stays which so materially hinder the circulation of water over square

Liver, the only locomotive built by Bury for the Liverpool & Manchester, was something of a hybrid with Stephenson outside frames and a Bury dome-topped boiler and firebox.

A classic Bury 2-2-0 'coaching' engine, such as No. 96 of the London & Birmingham Railway, built by Bury, Curtis & Kennedy in 1846 with 14-inch cylinders. Withdrawn from frontline service in 1869, she was cut up in 1880.

fireboxes, and the disposition of the fire-tubes [in an arc] such as to ensure their constantly being covered with water.

Armengaud et Armengaud described the firebox of Bury's *La Seine,* built for the Chemin de Fer de Paris à St Germaine in 1836:

> All the lateral surface, except where it meets the assemblage of the tubes, is in the form of a vertical cylinder, and at the bottom is the circular fireplace ... The upper part is a convex surface, which while presenting a little more heating surface [than a square fire box] also presents great solidity against the pressure of the water and steam. This form avoids the angles which are placed where the vertical and horizontal plates meet, when the firebox is rectangular (Armengaud & Armengaud, 1839: 125).

In a circular issued in 1842, Bury, Curtis & Kennedy stated the fireboxes of their early locomotives had reached their largest practical size necessary; that larger fireboxes were neither economical or fuel efficient; and moreover the round-topped firebox was safer:

> First, it is much safer than the square firebox, being made nearly in that shape which an excess of pressure beyond its stiffness would tend to bring it ... moreover, the strength of a square firebox is nearly dependent, individually of each of the stays fixed in it ... whereas pressure in a round firebox is borne equally by the whole area of the plates of which it is composed; again, corners in the square firebox, in which combustion is always languid, and consequently injurious, are avoided in a round firebox.
>
> A lead plug is placed at the culminant point of the round firebox, and therefore will melt before any other part is left dry ... but in a firebox with a flat top, the melting of the lead would only occur when the whole surface was dry.

In the specification he sent out to various sub-contractors, Bury specified that fireboxes were to be made from 'the best Yorkshire plate', either ⅜-inch Low Mow or Bowling, the firebox itself being welded rather than riveted so as not to have either rivet heads or lap joints exposed to the fire. Furthermore, a welded firebox was of a uniform thickness, 'the riveted joints, in effect, presenting a double thickness of metal', which could cause localised cool-spots, and the rivet heads 'not resisting for a very long time the intense heat of the fire to which they are exposed'.

The tubeplate was half an inch thick and the boiler barrel rolled from ⁵⁄₁₆-inch 'Yorkshire plate'. The outer firebox was lagged with mahogany strips, secured by two hoops; the dome of the firebox was covered with copper sheeting. Three try-cocks as well as a gauge glass (with lamp) were fitted as standard. The top of the outer firebox was surmounted by a lock-up safety valve. A second safety valve was usually provided on the first ring of the boiler. The regulator was mounted in the steam space formed by the high crown of the outer firebox. Bury's early regulators used a tapered plug valve which was worked in and out via a helical guide for the regulator handle. According to Flachat & Petiet it was impossible to keep the stuffing-box steamtight; it was difficult to lubricate; and in case of emergency the regulator could not be slammed shut as on a Stephenson locomotive. Furthermore the regulator valve itself did not necessarily shut properly due to differential expansion of the plug and valve seat as they got warm.

The domed crown of the inner firebox was originally made from two plates with a longitudinal seam, but these proved troublesome in service: *Coppernob*'s inner firebox is made from four plates and the domed crown (which is a later in-service replacement)

Above left: Detail of *Coppernob*'s cab fittings and tall, dome-topped firebox casing. While Bury's D-plan fireboxes were at first larger than contemporary Stephenson designs, they could not be as easily increased in size as rectangular fireboxes. (Douglas Roberts)

Above right: The Furness Railway had a suite of Bury type locomotives built by both Bury, Curtis & Kennedy of Liverpool and William Fairbairn of Manchester. Furness Railway No. 9 was built by Fairbairn in 1855.

Victoria, an 0-4-2 built by William Fairbairn for the Manchester, Bolton & Bury Railway, later became part of the Lancashire & Yorkshire Railway.

The 0-4-0 Bury type was the mainstay of the Manchester & Leeds Railway (latterly Lancashire & Yorkshire Railway) during the 1840s.

is supported by four wrought-iron roof bars. It is connected to the outer firebox by eight sling-stays. The outer firebox is made from twelve individual plates – the vertical section is made from four plates, while the complicated domed crown is made from eight. The boiler barrel is Low Moor iron, made in three rings lap-jointed together with a single line of rivets.

While it is true that the fireboxes of his early locomotives were much larger than the contemporary Stephenson products, the square firebox could be easily enlarged in length, height and width in order to exploit the maximum width between the outside frames. The circular firebox, as Charles Beyer noted in 1843, had probably reached its maximum size because of the use of inside frames – which had to be cranked around the firebox – on the standard gauge of 4 feet 8½ inches. A 4-foot diameter outer firebox was probably as big as Bury & Co. could build within existing design limits. The last use of the cylindrical firebox was an order for twenty 2-2-2 locomotives for Ireland in 1847; rectangular fireboxes were adopted a year later. Robert Fairlie, the designer of the articulated locomotive of the same name, however, re-adopted the Bury-style D-plan firebox in 1869.

Bury, Curtis & Kennedy were pioneers of high-pressure boilers: *Coppernob* of 1846 had a boiler pressure of 110 psi – higher than that of any contemporary Stephenson locomotive – and this combined with 14 x 24-inch cylinders gave a tractive effort of 7,617 lbs. Weighing nearly 18 tons (minus tender), *Coppernob* is thus neither 'small' nor 'puny', as the products of the Clarence Foundry have often been described.

Frames and Wheels

Bury's wrought-iron bar frames gave the engines a 'spindly' look compared to those of other builders. Bury specified the upper frame members to be formed from 4 x 1¾-inch iron bar while the lower member was round bar 1¾ inches in diameter. By the time *Coppernob* was built in 1846 the frames had been 'beefed up' a little: the upper members of *Coppernob*'s frame are formed from 4 x 2-inch flat iron bar while the lower members are 2-inch diameter round bar. On later six-wheeled locomotives, the frames were sturdier again at 4¼ x 2¼ inches, increasing in width over the wheels to 4¾ inches. Where the frame was joggled around the curve of the outer firebox, the proportions of the frame were inverted to 2 x 4¼ inches, the lower member being 2 x 3 inches. This bulge in the frames

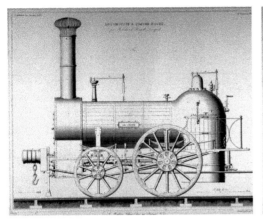

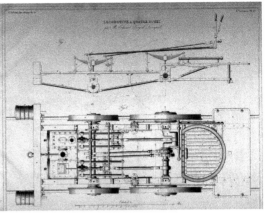

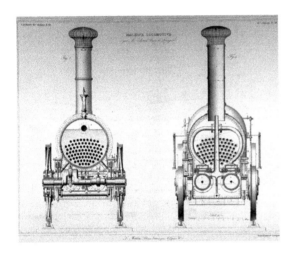

Above left, above right and left: *La Seine* (and three sisters, *Bury, Paris* and *Aigle*) was built by Bury, Curtis & Kennedy for the Chemin de Fer de Paris à St Germaine in 1836. She is typical of a mid-1830s Bury type locomotive.

to accommodate the cylindrical firebox in a six-wheeled locomotive was perhaps a major weak point in the design.

The two sides of the frame were joined by five transverse braces: a large C-shaped brace at the rear encompassing the firebox; in the centre by a transverse rod 1¾ inches in diameter which supported the ends of the slide bars; two 3¾ x 1-inch straps which supported the cylinders; and at the front by an oak buffer beam 14 x 7 inches thick. The cylinders were securely bolted to the outside frames so that the thrust past through the frames. Two wrought-iron brackets supported the boiler which, as with the Stephenson locomotive, was considered the main structural element of the locomotive. At that time it was not understood that boilers expand when under pressure and no expansion brackets were fitted, which, despite the modest pressures then in use, must have put considerable strain on the boiler, which would have ultimately developed a 'hog's back' shape. The draw bar was attached to the rear C-shaped member, rather than being riveted to the back of the firebox.

Like Stephenson, Bury used composite wheels. The nave was cast solid, into which cylindrical wrought-iron spokes with tapered ends were fitted into tapered holes drilled into the casting and secured by keys, driven in from the outside face of the nave. The spokes were offset, like on a bicycle wheel, to give lateral strength. The rim of the wheel was ⅝ inches thick, to which were riveted forged iron T-shaped brackets which connected with the outer end of the spoke. A tyre was shrunk on to the rim. The success of Bury's wheel design is shown by the Directors of the Liverpool & Manchester preferring them (or those of Richard Roberts & Co.) overs those of Stephenson.

The firm adopted inside axle boxes and dispensed with the intermediate plate frames and their attendant bearings in order to reduce the rolling friction of the chassis – and because he did not believe that the five or six bearings of a Stephenson locomotive could be kept perfectly true. Flachat & Petiet, however, concluded:

> In the four-wheeled engines of Mr. Bury ... the whole assemblage has an appearance of lightness because the wheels are outside the frames; but this reduces the solidity of the whole. The outside framed engine relies on the cross-braces at the front and back to make it rigid ... the absence of an outside frame, and the strong cross-braces, has no advantage in decreasing rolling friction. The crank axle is not as solidly supported without bearings in the middle, and is supported only at its extremities. The parallelism of the axle is difficult to maintain. (Flachat & Petiet, 1840: 119–120)

Furthermore, the two Frenchmen concluded that if an axle broke, particularly the cranked driving axle with its numerous points of weakness, then the engine would derail as the axle was only supported on two points. On a Stephenson locomotive, a broken cranked axle would still be supported on several points, but this came at the expense of increased complication. Other French authorities describe how the use of outside wheels and inside frames made maintenance, and in particular lubrication of axle boxes and springs, difficult. That said, Bury was clearly a man ahead of his time in advocating inside frames rather than outside sandwich frames, features which gradually began to disappear from the late 1840s onwards with the adoption of inside plate (rather than bar) frames and outside wheels with only two bearings per axle.

Popular opinion turned against four-wheeled locomotives in the light of the appalling accident just outside Paris at Meudon on the Chemin de Fer Paris à Versailles Rive Gauche on 8 May 1842. The train was hauled by two locomotives: a six-wheel Patentee piloted by a 2-2-0 Planet type. The leading axle of the Planet broke at speed, causing the engine to derail; the train engine and coaches continued over the mangled Planet, resulting in a catastrophic accident, where passengers who were locked inside their carriages burned to death. The following inquest came to the conclusion that four-wheeled locomotives were more likely to derail if an axle broke, but in both instances 'there were the most grave consequences' if an axle broke on any type of locomotive. Ultimately, four versus six wheels on a locomotive was 'still a problem to solve'. The inquest referred to an experiment made by Bury:

> The reason for the preference put forward by Mr Bury, for the inside frame, is that in the case of the rupture of an axle, the weight of the engine supports the flanges of the wheels against the rails, and there is little chance of it coming off the rails. He carried out an experiment on this subject on the London & Birmingham Railway, travelling a great distance, without accident, with a cut-through axle. (Mathias, 1844: 187–188)

The experiment referred to took place on 23 June 1842; Bury had the leading axle of 2-2-0 No. 18 partly sawn through close to one of the journals, leaving only a 1-inch thickness. He ran the engine until the axle broke. On 24 June, and with a load of 32 tons, Bury ran the engine – still with a broken axle — at 25 mph from Wolverton to Watford, where one of the leading wheels left the rails. The wheel came off the rails and was put back on again near Harrow and in both cases the engine did not leave the rails. While noting the success of Bury's experiment, the Académie des Sciences suggested that in order to prove his claim of superior safety, a similar experiment should be repeated with a six-wheeled locomotive.

Despite the success of his experiment, the Paris accident set popular opinion in France and Britain against four-wheeled locomotives – a situation made worse for Bury when a 2-2-0 of Bury type by Hick & Co. broke its front axle in December of the same year, derailing and resulting in the death of a female passenger. Such was the concern in France that a bill was proposed in the *Parlement* to ban the use of four-wheel engines in France entirely, and many French railways converted their four-wheelers to six-wheelers in light of the Meudon accident. Within weeks of the accident, the Liverpool & Manchester Railway banned four-wheel engines piloting six-wheelers.

Valve Gear

Bury's earliest locomotives used slip-eccentric valve gear, as described by Flachat & Petiet (1840). While Stephenson locomotives had limited-travel slip-eccentrics that could be moved laterally between a pair of 'driving dogs' which engaged into a slot on the eccentric cheeks, Bury used a 'driving pin forged on the axle itself', which did not 'enter into the eccentrics, but rests only against them'. In other words, the eccentric ran round until the 'stop' on the eccentric cluster engaged with the 'driving-pin' or 'stop' on the driving axle – one stop for fore-gear and a second for back. The eccentric rods terminated with drop hooks which could be raised or lowered from pins on a rocking arm which drove the valve spindles. As with a Stephenson locomotive, the valves were free to be set by hand until they were locked into place. To get the locomotive moving, it would have to be 'driven on the handles' in order for the eccentrics to run round and find the correct 'stop' on the axle. Because there was no reversing pedal it was difficult at a glance to tell which direction – if any – the locomotive would move off in: Flachat & Petiet note that in most cases they moved off in reverse! Nor were the valve levers on the footplate any indication of direction of travel; the left-hand valve lever controlled the right-hand valve and the right-hand lever the left-hand valve. To make matters worse, when the lever was in its forward position, the valve was at the back of its travel. This was the opposite of the simple Stephenson system where the left-hand lever moved the left-hand valve, and when the lever was forward, so was the valve.

In his later locomotives, Bury adopted a version of the Stephenson 'flying reverse', wherein the eccentric cluster was free to move laterally on the driving axle between two stops forged on the axle, the movement being controlled with a sprung foot-pedal à la Stephenson. On the footplate were three levers: two worked the valves directly, while the third lowered or raised the drop-hooks.

Edward Bury's 1838 circular shows the use of four fixed eccentrics, the eccentric rods ending in drop-hooks. There were three levers on the footplate: one raised or lowered the drop-hooks, simultaneously engaging one pair while the other disengaged. The other two controlled the valves, and, as with the earlier valve gear, the movement of the valve levers was contrary to that of the valves. Unlike a Stephenson locomotive, where most of the valve gear was actually outside the frames and readily accessible, Edward Bury utilised the space between the frames, where it must have made maintenance problematic. Bury was an early adopter of the Stephenson-Howe link motion, with *Coppernob* being supplied with it in 1846.

Locomotives for Home

Bury's first locomotive for the Liverpool & Manchester Railway was delivered in 1832. Named *Liver*, Ahrons (1923) suggests she was the first locomotive by Bury & Co. for the home market. *Liver* was one of two engines ordered in August 1831, and was delivered in January 1832 at a cost of £750. She was built to the Planet design of Stephenson & Co. with an outside sandwich frame but carried Bury's typical D-plan firebox. She had driving wheels 5 feet in diameter and 11 x 18-inch cylinders. The second locomotive was sold to John Hargreaves, lessee of the Bolton & Leigh Railway, upon delivery in April 1832. Two more engines were ordered from Bury by the L&M in summer 1832: one was sold to the Bolton & Leigh Railway, and the other, with 5-foot 6-inch diameter wheels, was supplied to Messrs Bourne & Robinson, but because of her large wheels she was only allowed to run at a very slow speed on the L&M. *Liver* was fitted with a new firebox in November 1834 and during 1836–37 was the testbed for a patent 'double firebox' designed to burn coal and coke by John and William Gray, an experiment which sadly ended in tragedy when the mid-feather between each firebox burst, severely scalding the engineman, Joseph Derbyshire. The fireman, William Wood, had his thigh broken.

It was on the Liverpool & Manchester that considerable controversy arose over the shape of firebox to be used. George Stephenson believed Bury's fireboxes were 'objectionable and dangerous, as they could not be advantageously strengthened by cross stays as the square sided fireboxes were' – not that a dome-topped cylindrical firebox needed stays. In early July 1832 the Board ordered 'a survey by two Boilermakers be held on the fireplaces of Mr Bury's engines, to ascertain whether their mode of construction is safe'. One of the boilermakers was to be appointed by Bury, and the second by the L&M. They reported to the Board at the end of July, and George Stephenson presented his case in September. Because of the 'decided difference of opinion' between Bury and Stephenson, and because several of Bury's engines were running on their line, the Directors resolved to 'request the professional opinion of John Farey Esq. of London' on the matter. Bury and Stephenson were also requested to put their views in writing.

John Farey Jnr (1791–1851) was a noted mechanical engineer and the author of a two-volume treatise on steam engines (1827). Bury immediately objected; he thought that there should be at least six expert witnesses, half chosen by the Board and half by himself. As a result, the Board consented to allow Farey to consult 'two other *impartial* Engineers of acknowledged ability' to be chosen by him. Farey, therefore, consulted Joshua Field FRS (1786–1863), one of the founders of the Institution of Civil Engineers and a member of the Royal Society. The two reported to the Board in January 1833, arguing that as the 'circular fireplace' was not a true cylinder, and because it had a flat top without any stays – having to rely solely 'on the stiffness of the metal' to prevent it collapsing – it was not as a safe a

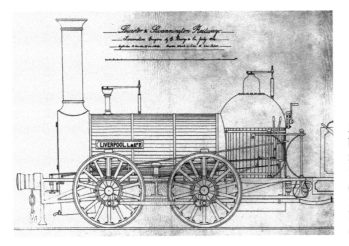

Liverpool (No. 7) was built for the Leicester & Swannington Railway in 1834. She featured 4-foot 6-inch driving wheels and 12 x 20-inch cylinders. The boiler had 2-inch outside diameter tubes.

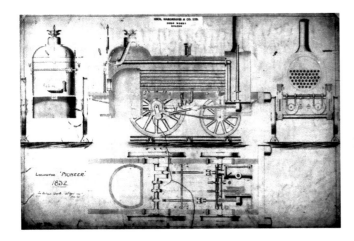

Pioneer was a Bury-type built by Hick, Hargreaves & Co. of Bolton in 1832. Unusually, she had inside sandwich frames rather than the bar frames more typical of Bury locomotives.

rectangular box, which could be 'advantageously' stayed to prevent collapse. They thought that stays between inner and outer fireboxes, however, could impair the flow of water, and also that a firebox with stays was more likely to leak due to 'unequal expansion of the metal plates'. In order to make Bury's fireboxes safe, Farey and Field recommended fitting crown stays and girders to them. They concluded that square fireboxes were safer because they could be stayed; that they had a larger grate area; were smaller and lighter and therefore made for a better-balanced engine; and could be more easily enlarged in size. In light of this report, the Directors' Minutes note:

> Read Mr Farey's and Mr. Joshua Field's Report on the comparative advantages and disadvantages of Round and Square Fire Places for Loco-Motive engines; and giving a decided preference to the Square Firebox, principally on the score of superior safety. (RAIL 371/3)

Edward Bury objected to the conclusion drawn by Farey and Field; he argued that an incorrect drawing of the firebox of *Liver* had been sent to London. Furthermore, he had made 'an alteration and improvement in the form of his circular firebox' (probably sling stays between the inner and outer fireboxes) which, if Farey had known of them, 'would have [been] induced to alter his opinion'. An exasperated Henry Booth tried to placate Bury, requesting he put down his grievances in writing so they could be forwarded to Farey and Field, and that any differences between the drawings of *Liver* and the actual engine be looked into. Finally, Bury wrote to the board 'declining to interfere further in the discussion or decision respecting round or square fire-places.'

But this was not the end of Bury & Co.'s involvement with the L&M; in March 1833 Bury speculatively offered to build two large luggage engines, but the offer was declined, while in December the Board wrote to Bury inviting him to tender for two goods engines 'with coupled wheels, with copper firebox, brass tubes, and other particulars to be specified'. Bury & Co.'s tender of £1,140 each, however, was the highest of those submitted: the lowest, of Charles Tayleur & Co. for £950, was accepted.

Bury & Co. built 415 locomotives between 1830 and 1850, when the firm failed. 180 of these were supplied to the London & Birmingham Railway, of which Edward Bury was both the sole contractor for motive power, locomotive superintendent and also private locomotive manufacturer. This was a position he held thanks to a powerful group of Liverpool-based Directors of the London & Birmingham led by the Quaker Edward Cropper who resented the influence of father-and-son team George and Robert Stephenson on the Liverpool & Manchester (of which Cropper was also a Director), and were opposed to monopolies of any sort, which he believed the Stephensons enjoyed on the L&M. Bury & Co. did not enjoy an outright monopoly on locomotives built for the London & Birmingham, supplying 110 of them, the rest coming from other outside firms. However, all 180 were

Furness Railway No. 14, a classic Bury type 0-4-0 built by William Fairbairn of Manchester as late as 1858 – not bad for a design from the early 1830s!

Furness Railway No. 13 by Fairbairn entered service in 1858 and was withdrawn in 1900.

Furness Railway No. 16 of 1861 was the last of two Bury type locomotives to be delivered.

An Edwardian postcard showing Furness Railway No. 3 (*Coppernob*) coupled to old four-wheeled Victorian carriages in order to recreate the earliest passenger trains on that line.

Built by Bury, Curtis & Kennedy in 1848 for the Great Southern & Western Railway of Ireland, No. 36 worked until 1896, when she was preserved. She is currently on display at Cork Kent railway station.

built to Bury's standard design, and the Clarence Foundry also supplied track components such as switches and turn tables. The Manchester, Bolton & Bury, Manchester & Leeds, Leeds & Selby, Midland Counties Railway, Furness Railway and the Great Northern all used Bury-type locomotives.

And Abroad

Bury & Co.'s rebuff from the Liverpool & Manchester led to them exploring the lucrative export market. Their fifth locomotive – *Roanoke* – was built for the United States and marks the beginning of not only a profitable period for the company, but of classic features of the American locomotive for much of the nineteenth century, incorporating the use of bar frames and a D-plan dome-topped firebox. Built for the Petersburg Railroad in 1832, *Roanoke* was a four-coupled locomotive with 4-foot 6-inch driving wheels and 8 x 16-inch cylinders, set low down under the smokebox and angled upwards so that the connecting rods passed under the leading axle. Boiler pressure was 50 psi and the safety-valve was 'locked off' at 65 psi. The boiler barrel was 6 feet 9 inches long and 3 feet in diameter – far larger than that of the contemporary Stephenson Planet type. A further four locomotives for the Petersburg Railroad (two 0-4-0s and one 2-2-0) were ordered from Bury & Co. in 1833–34.

Bury's sixth and seventh locomotives (*Comet* and *Catawissa*) were also for export, intended for the Little Schuylkill Navigation Railroad & Coal Co. in January 1833. Meanwhile, their eighth locomotive was *Liverpool,* for the Petersburg Railroad. In total the Clarence Foundry supplied twenty locomotives to the United States between 1830 and 1840; Messrs Braithwaite, Milner & Co. of London sent a further sixteen locomotives of the same 'Bury' type.

Bury & Co. supplied four locomotives (*Bury, Paris, L'Aigle* and *La Seine*) to France for the Chemin de Fer de Paris à St Germaine, which opened in August 1837. One of these locos appeared on a commemorative medallion struck to celebrate the occasion.

Four Wheels Good, Six Wheels Bad

Edward Bury is usually depicted Canute-like, trying to hold back the rising tide of six-wheeled locomotives. In their circular of 1842, Bury, Curtis & Kennedy set out logical reasoning for maintaining four-wheeled locomotives:

> The four-wheel engine is less costly than that on six wheels; it can be got into less space; it is much lighter, and therefore requires less power to take it up the inclines, and consequently leaves more available power to take up the train; is safer, as it adapts itself better to the rails, not being so likely to run off the lines at curves or crossings; is more economical in the working, there being fewer parts in motion and less friction; those parts of the machinery which are common to both plans are more easily got at in the four-wheeled engine; the buildings and turntables are not required to be on so large a scale; as there are fewer parts in the four-wheeled engine, fewer tools, as lathes, drills & c. are required; having fewer parts to be deranged, stoppages are not so likely.

Bury's criticisms of the six-wheeled engine's poor weight distribution were valid; it presented little improvement on a well-balanced four-wheel engine with weight equally distributed between both axles. A four-wheeled engine was easier on the track, and with a shorter wheel base than a six-wheeled engine, could travel around tighter curves. Bury's major criticism of the six-wheeled engine was that it only existed 'in the necessity of supporting the large and heavy firebox, which was not sufficiently balanced at the smokebox end'. Therefore, there was 'no such necessity' with a well-balanced four-wheeled engine. Furthermore, more weight was available for adhesion via two rather than three axles, and in a four-coupled engine total weight was available.

This was a debate which was followed closely abroad. Monsieur Petiet of the Chemin de Fer de Paris à Versailles Rive Gauche agreed with Bury about the poor weight distribution of six-wheeled engines, arguing the leading axle was more prone to breakages than that of a four-wheeler, but he could not be drawn on which was safer. Monsieur Séguier of the Académie de Sciences preferred four-coupled four-wheeled locomotives because they had total weight available for adhesion and had a balanced weight distribution.

The *Journal des Chemins de Fer* (12 February 1842) opined that the six-wheeled locomotive was neither more nor less intrinsically safer than the four-wheeler as any locomotive could be involved in a collision; the safety of a locomotive and its train was dependent upon the locomotive and train crew rather than the number of wheels the engine possessed. But, if involved in an accident it was the strength of the framing of the engine which was more important. Four- and six-wheeled locomotives were both subject to 'lateral vibration and oscillation' which was not dependent on the number of wheels; six-wheel locomotives (from their longer wheelbase) were considered more damaging to the permanent way, especially going around curves at speed, than four-wheelers, the latter being able to handle sharper curves and more lightly laid track better; and finally, both four- and six-wheel locomotives were equally likely to come off the track if the leading wheel or crank axle broke. Where the *Journal* did find criticism with the six-wheeled locomotive was in weight distribution: four-coupled four-wheelers had all their weight available for adhesion, more or less evenly distributed. Six-wheeled engines, however, were found to carry as much as 50 per cent of their weight on their driving wheels, but with the leading wheels too heavily loaded. This put excessive strain on the leading axle, especially going round curves. Because the driving wheels had no flanges, the leading and trailing wheels took the lateral strain going in and out of curves, making the chances of a broken leading axle more likely. The six-wheeler did have an advantage in that it was generally bigger than a four-wheeler, with a larger boiler and firebox, and therefore could be worked more economically. The *Journal* concluded with a Gallic shrug:

> Where the trains are light and frequent, small locomotives with four wheels are the best, but small locomotives will be found to be more expensive to purchase and maintain than larger locomotives for proportionate power.

Four-wheel engines with round fireboxes had probably reached their maximum size limit, whereas the six-wheeled engine still had capacity to increase in size thanks to the use of the square firebox. Four to six wheels had been a natural evolution but it did not mean one wheel arrangement was superior to the other. As the *Journal de Chemins de Fer* concluded, it was a matter of 'horses for courses': four-wheeled engines were good at some tasks, especially on light track with sharp cures, while six-wheeled engines were better at others, usually running fast on relatively straight track.

Small and Puny?

Despite usually being written off by later historians as 'small and puny', these were sturdy, compact locomotives which performed well with the loads asked of them. They were built to handle the light loads (up to 50 tons) of the short trains of the early 1830s, and were successful in that role. They were not small or puny, having larger boilers and fireboxes than contemporary Stephenson locomotives. The French admired their standardisation and interchangeability of parts as well as the quality of their finish, finding them superior to anything produced by Stephenson & Co. at Forth Street. The quality of build and materials is exemplified in the longevity of these engines, having a working life of over a decade or more while a Stephenson Planet or Patentee had a working life half of that: *Coppernob* (Furness Railway No. 3) and her sister No. 4 worked from 1846 until 1898, in ostensibly original condition. Similarly, No. 36, which was built for the Great Southern & Western Railway in Ireland in 1848, ran until 1896, when it was preserved, also largely in original condition.

Conclusion

The period from 1830 to 1855 was world-changing. The locomotive had evolved from a curiosity to an everyday part of life; public railways had grown from more than a hundred miles to several thousand, and were found on just about every continent on the globe. The pace and amount of change – technologically and in society – was dramatic, affecting just about every aspect of daily life. Steam power, and the railways, were here to stay.

In 1829 *Rocket* was cutting-edge technology, reaching unheard of speeds of 15, or even 20 mph. Yet, within a year of her delivery she was obsolete. *Planet* made a run between Liverpool and Manchester in 60 minutes, averaging 30 miles an hour. Locomotives not only got faster, but bigger: *Rocket* weighed less than 5 tons, *Planet* weighed 8 tons and by the end of our period *Iron Duke* weighed 41 tons. The pace of change was led through the enormous success of the railway as a means of communication and financial investment: the weight of traffic to be moved demanded faster, more powerful locomotives to work ever heavier and speedier trains.

This, of course, presented its own technological challenges. While the wood and iron wheels of *Rocket* and her sisters had been successful enough at relatively low speeds and power outputs, the similar wheels used on the first of the Planet class were prone to failure. In attempting to overcome this – and without a test track – Robert Stephenson and his Forth Street team came up with patent iron wheels, but these too presented problems in service, presenting an opportunity for other firms, such as Edward Bury of Liverpool or Charles Tayleur at the Vulcan Foundry, to develop their own iron wheels. In an age before James Nasmyth had developed the steam hammer, the forging of crank axles was also problematic: not only were the axles of the first Planet locomotives poorly designed, they were also poorly made, making them prone to failure– the failure of an axle often being coincident with the breaking of a wheel. Failure or partial failure of components resulted in several nasty accidents, but accidents from which lessons were learned, driving forward the development of axles and wheels, and therefore railway safety.

Making steam, too, presented its own metallurgical challenges. While the firebox of *Rocket* had been made entirely of copper, the increasing cost of copper had meant that the first Planet locomotives had iron fireboxes. Iron, being less conductive than copper, made them less efficient at producing steam, and perhaps due to the accumulation of scale due to poor boiler management, they were found to 'burn out' quickly. Copper inner fireboxes became the norm on the British steam locomotive from 1834 to the introduction of all-steel, all-welded fireboxes by Oliver Bulleid in the 1940s. Similarly, while copper boiler tubes had been successful enough on *Rocket*, in daily main line service they had been found to quickly wear out, leading at first to the introduction of thicker copper tubes, and finally brass.

The increasing size and weight of locomotives also presented another problem the engineers had to overcome: axle load. The track of the Liverpool & Manchester Railway had only been designed with a maximum axle load of 4½ tons in mind, yet *Planet* carried 5 tons on her driving wheels, and locomotives only got heavier as the railways became more successful. Thus the introduction of a third axle to create the Patentee type in 1833, and then a fourth by Gooch in the 1840s, was designed to overcome weight restrictions due to relatively lightweight wrought-iron rails laid primarily on rigid stone blocks (the GWR notwithstanding) into the 1850s – the development of the permanent track being sadly outside the scope of this book. Yet, for all its size, Gooch's *Iron Duke* was in its basic design an enlarged Stephenson Patentee, which would maintain that design for a further thirty years until the final abolition of the broad gauge. Against this background, Edward Bury does appear Canute-like, trying to stem the tide of six-wheeled locomotives. His earliest locomotives, however, were bigger and had larger heating surfaces than contemporary Stephenson products, and, unlike Forth Street, the Clarence Foundry produced standard locomotives using machine tools. The Clarence Foundry, Sharp, Roberts of Manchester, and even the Vulcan Foundry (Charles Tayleur) had made the technological leap from the blacksmith tradition of the early colliery locomotives to a modern, steam-powered workshop able to produce high-quality locomotives in relatively large numbers, leaving the pioneers at Forth Street lagging behind.

The locomotive had evolved rapidly from 1829 to 1855, and it is remarkable that in only thirty-three months from 1828 to 1830 Robert Stephenson and his team had developed the locomotive from a lumbering curiosity to the first 'class' of main line express passenger locomotive, the main design criteria of which would remain the basis of all subsequent locomotives until the delivery of Britain's last main line locomotive design in 1960.

Bibliography and Further Reading

Archival

The National Archives, Kew:
RAIL 351/3 Leeds & Selby Railway, Board of Directors' Minutes, 1830–1835.
RAIL 371/1 Liverpool & Manchester Railway, Board of Directors' Minutes, 1826–1830.
RAIL 371/2 Liverpool & Manchester, Board of Directors' Minutes, 1830–1833.
RAIL 371/3 Liverpool & Manchester Railway, Board of Directors' Minutes, 1833–1836.
RAIL 371/4 Liverpool & Manchester Railway, Board of Directors' Minutes, 1836–1838.
RAIL 371/5 Liverpool & Manchester Railway, Board of Directors' Minutes, 1838–1842.
RAIL 371/8 Liverpool & Manchester Railway, Management Committee. Minutes, 1831–1833.
RAIL 371/10 Liverpool & Manchester Railway, Management Committee. Minutes, 1833–1839.
RAIL 371/11 Liverpool & Manchester Railway, Management Committee. Minutes, 1839–1845.
RAIL 371/40 Liverpool & Manchester Railway, Performances of Locomotives and Coke Consumption, 1839–1840.
RAIL 1008/88/1 Report of George and Robert Stephenson on Motive Power, 1828–1829.
RAIL 1008/88/4 Letters from Robert Stephenson to Henry Booth Regarding Construction of *Rocket*, 1829.

The National Railway Museum, York:
NRM 1998-8764 John Melling Papers.
NRM ROB/2/1/1 Robert Stephenson & Co. Order Book No. 1, March 1832.
ROB/2/2/2 Robert Stephenson & Co., List of engines finished.
ROB/2/3/1 Robert Stephenson & Co., List of engines delivered.
ROB/3/2/ Robert Stephenson & Co., locomotive drawings, Nos 14–25, Nos 31–33.

Primary

Anon, *Description des Locomotives Stephenson circulant sur les chemins de fer en Angleterre, et en France, et ... Bruxelles* (Bruxelles: J-B Champeron, 1835).

Armengaud & Armengaud, *L'Industrie des Chemins De Fer* (Paris: L. Mathias, 1839).

Colburn, Z., *Locomotive Engineering and the Mechanics of Railways* (London: William Collins, Sons & Co., 1877).

Clark, D. K., 'On the improvement of Railway Locomotive Stock', in *Minutes of the Proceedings of the Institute of Civil Engineers*, Vol. XVI (1856–57), pp. 3–43.

Clark, D. K., *Railway Machinery* (London: Blackie, 1855).

Farey, J. and J. Field, 'Report of John Farey and Joshua Field: Respecting Boilers for Steam Engines', *The Artizan*, Vol. 3, pp. 19–20.

Flachat E., and J. Petiet, *Guide du Mécanicien Conducteur des Machines Locomotive* (Paris: Mathias, 1840).

Marshall, W. P., *Description of the Patent Locomotive Engine of Robert Stephenson* (London: John Weale, 1838).

Mathias, F., *Études sur les Machines Locomotives de Sharp et Roberts, comparée à celle d'autres constructeurs* (Paris: L. Mathias, 1844).

'Melling's Patent for Improvements in Steam Engines', *The Repertory of Patent Inventions*, No. LV (July 1838), pp. 1–11.

'Messrs Bury & Co.'s Circular', *The Mechanics' Magazine*, Vol. XXXVIII (January – July 1843), pp. 199–204.

de Pambour, F. M. G., *Traité théorique et pratique des machines locomotives* (Paris: Bachelier, 1840). 2e édition.

Recollection of Edward Bury by his widow (John Garnet, nd).

Shaw, I., *Views of the most interesting scenery on the line of the Liverpool & Manchester Railway* (Liverpool: I. Shaw, 1831).

'Stephenson's Patent for an Improvement in Locomotive Steam Engines', *The Repertory of Patent Inventions*, No. XI (November 1834), pp. 260–270.

'The 'Albert' or Model Four-Wheeled Locomotive', *The Mechanics Magazine*, vol. XXXVII (July – December 1842), pp. 450–455.

Walker, J. S., *An Accurate Description of the Liverpool & Manchester Railway* (Liverpool: J. F. Cannell, 1830).

Secondary

Anon, 'Locomotives supplied by British Firms to American Railroads. Part III', *The Engineer* (March 11 1898).

Anon, 'Locomotives supplied by British Firms to American Railroads. Part IV', *The Engineer* (March 18 1898).

Ahrons, E. L., 'Short histories of famous firms: Edward Bury & Co.', *The Engineer* (February 2 1923).

Bailey, M. R., ed., *Robert Stephenson – The Eminent Engineer* (London: Routledge, 2017).

Bailey, M. R., *Loco Motion. The world's oldest steam locomotives* (Stroud: The History Press, 2014).

Bailey, M. R., 'Leaning Through Replication: The *Planet* Project' in *Transactions of the Newcomen Society*, Vol. 68 (1996–1997), pp. 109–136.

Bailey M. R. and J. P. Glithero, *The Engineering and History of Rocket* (London: The Science Museum, 2001).

Bailey, M. R., 'Robert Stephenson & Co. 1823–1829', *Transactions of the Newcomen Society*, Vol. 50, (1979–1980), pp. 252–291.

Booth, H., *Henry Booth. Inventor; Partner in the Rocket; Father of Railway Management* (Ilfracombe: Arthur H. Stockwell Ltd, 1980).

Bourne, J., 'Recollections of Improvements which had been made in the Steam Engine in the last half century, No. IV', *The Engineer* (24 December 1875).

Claussen, P., 'Edward Bury's first sixteen locomotives', *Backtrack*, Vol. 32, No. 10 (October 2018), pp. 620–623.

Dawson, A. L., 'Planet: instructions not included', *The L&NWR Society Journal*, Vol. 9, No. 3 (December 2018), pp. 110–123.

Dawson, A. L., *The Rainhill Trials* (Stroud: Amberley Publishing, 2018).

Dawson, A. L., *The Early Railways of Leeds* (Stroud: Amberley Publishing, 2018).

Dawson, A. L., *Lion's Tale: Designing, Building and Operating Lion.* Key-note address, Old Locomotive Committee, Liverpool Museum 14 April 2018.

Dawson, A. L., 'Lion: the Cinderella Engine', *Steam Railway*, No. 476 (February 2018), pp. 38–42.

Dawson, A. L., *Planet, Lion and Burys: Experiences of early Locomotive Management* paper presented to The L&NWR Society, Kidderminster Railway Museum, 29 July 2017.

Dendy Marshall, C. F., *A History of Railway Locomotives down to the end of the year 1831* (London: Locomotive Publishing Co., 1953).

Fancy, W. F., 'An Old Locomotive', *The Railway Magazine*, Vol. IV (Jan–June 1899), pp. 217–218.

Hills, Dr R. L., 'The development of machine tools in the early railway era', in. M. R. Bailey, ed., *Early Railways 3* (Sudbury: Six Martlets, 2006), pp. 242–259.

Hills, Dr R. L., and D. Patrick, *Beyer Peacock: Locomotive Builders to the World* (Glossop: Transport Publishing Co., 1982).

Jack, H., *Locomotives of the LNWR Southern Division* (RCTS, 2001).

Owen, T., *The Great Survivor: the Rebirth of a Victorian Engine* (Furness Railways Trust, nd).

Stuart D. H., and B. Reed, *The Crewe Type. Loco Profile 15* (Windsor: Profile Publications Ltd, 1971).

Platt, A., *The Life and times of Daniel Gooch* (Gloucester: Alan Sutton Ltd, 1987).

Warren, J. G. H., *Century of Locomotive Building by Robert Stephenson & Co.* (Andrew Reid & Co., 1923).

Journals

Herapath's Railway Journal
Journal des Chemins de Fer
The Engineer
The Mechanics' Magazine
The Railway Magazine